ALPACA ♡ ♡ ♡

need. more. yarn. now.

Frida Pontén

MOHAIR ♥ ♥ ♥

KNITTING
FOR THE FUN OF IT

TS

TRAFALGAR SQUARE
North Pomfret, Vermont

First published in the United States of America in 2018 by
Trafalgar Square Books
North Pomfret, Vermont 05053

Originally published in Norwegian as *Fridas fargesirkus*.

Copyright © 2016 Cappelen Damm AS
English translation © 2018 Trafalgar Square Books

ISBN: 978-1-57076-882-8

Library of Congress Control Number: 2018936219

Book Design: Frida Pontén
Interior Layout: Laila Sundet Gundersen
Photography: Leif Hansen
Translation into Norwegian: Toril Blomquist
Drawings and Charts: Frida Pontén
Translation into English: Carol Huebscher Rhoades

Printed in China
10 9 8 7 6 5 4 3 2 1

CONTENTS

F as in Freedom

Welcome to my yarn circus!

I want my work to be a tribute to everything and everyone not content to be cut from the same cloth: those that don't always follow the rules, those that like to step outside the box—of everything! To all that is imperfect and artistic and lovely, bohemian and wild and a little whimsical; and, above all, to everyone who dares to go their own way!

This book is for all those who love creativity and think it is exciting to see what they can make with their own hands. I know I really love the process of bringing a work to life, and there's no substitute for the feeling of being able to choose and decide for myself how a project should look.

Now that I've worked full-time with clothing and furnishing design for large companies, it's become important to me that what I make on my own time doesn't look bought or mass-produced. I like it best when things are a little out of balance, so anyone can see that the result was handmade with love. Things don't need to be error-free to be beautiful! "Bless the mess"— that's my mantra. And it should go without saying, but freedom is actually the most important aspect of my own life and my creative development. That no one can say, "Stop!" or tell me what I want to do isn't possible. No, no brakes here—just drive on, that's what I say!

I hope you'll find many projects and ideas in this book that you think are appealing and exciting, that you'll have fun, and that you can find happiness in expressing your own creativity along the way. So don't feel bound by the instructions: purl instead of knitting, use a different yarn, or find colors you like better! Do whatever you want to do to make these designs your own. Enjoy!

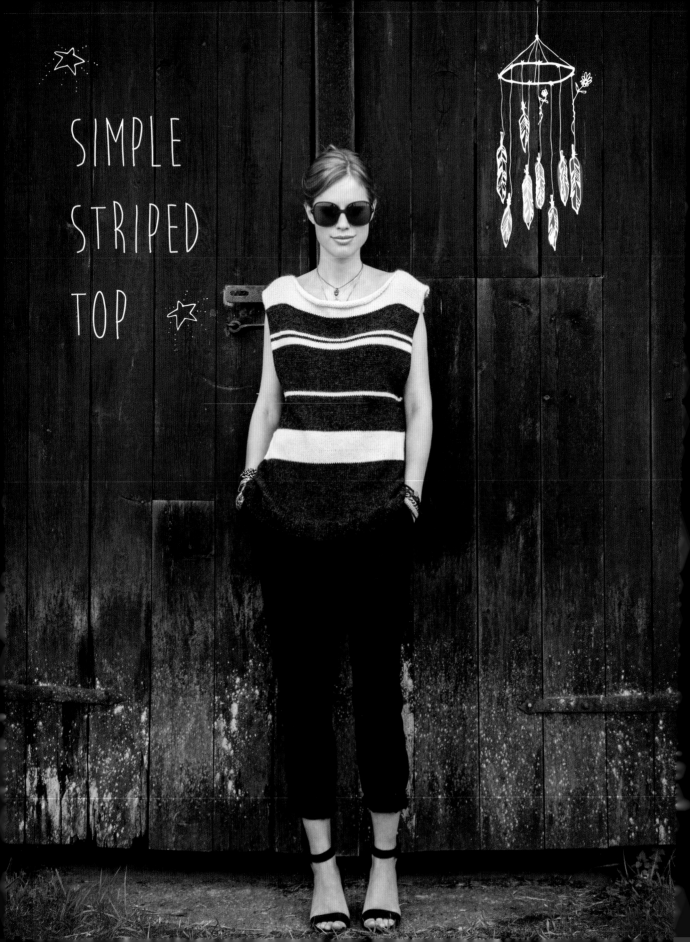

SIMPLE
STRIPED
TOP

HERE'S A KNITTED GARMENT YOU CAN MAKE WHILE SITTING IN FRONT OF THE TV— THAT'S HOW EASY IT IS! I KNITTED THE FRONT AND BACK SEPARATELY, BUT YOU CAN CHOOSE TO KNIT IT ALL IN ONE PIECE ON A CIRCULAR NEEDLE AND THEN DIVIDE FOR THE FRONT AND BACK WHEN YOU GET TO THE ARMHOLES. I WANTED A LOOSE AND FREE LOOK AT THE TOP, SO I USED NEEDLES U.S. SIZE 8 / 5 MM INSTEAD OF U.S. 4 / 3.5 MM AS SUGGESTED ON THE YARN BALL BAND.

LEVEL OF DIFFICULTY
Easy

SIZE
Measure and fit to desired size

MATERIALS
Yarn:
CYCA #3 (DK/light worsted) Sandnes Garn Alpakka (100% alpaca, 120 yd/110 m / 50 g)
Yarn Colors and Amounts:
Black 1099: 200 g
Pale Pink 3911: 100 g
My top weighed a total of 9 oz / 255 g.
Needles: U. S. size 8 / 5 mm

GAUGE
20 sts = 4 in / 10 cm
Adjust needle size to obtain correct gauge if necessary (or calculate your own stitch numbers).
I wanted to knit a top with a chest measurement of 39½ in / 100 cm, which meant 19¾ in / 50 cm each for front and back. Since my gauge is 20 sts per 4 in, my calculations were:
20 sts divided by 4 = 5 sts per inch x 19¾ in = 99 sts, rounded up to 100 sts each for front and back / 20 sts divided by 10 = 2 sts per cm x 50 cm = 100 sts each for front and back.

1. **Front:** With Black, CO 100 sts. Loosely work back and forth in k5, p5 ribbing for 4¼ in / 11 cm. This ribbing is loosely knitted as a finishing touch on the garment, and is not elastic.
2. BO all sts loosely. The loose bind-off on the front produces a soft, draping neckline at the front; the back neck is more firmly finished for a straight-across back neck.
3. Now work in stockinette and stripes. My stripe sequence was: 35 rows Black (not counting the ribbing), 18 rows Pink, 20 rows Black, 2 rows Pink, 26 rows Black, 4 rows Pink, 2 rows Black, 2 rows Pink, 16 rows Black, and 20 rows Pink.
4. **Back:** Work the back as for the front, binding off the neckline more tightly.
5. **Finishing:** Join the shoulders and seam the sides. I only sewed a few inches / centimeters for the shoulder seam, so my top has a wide boat neck.
6. Weave in all ends neatly on WS.
7. Soak the top in lukewarm water and then gently squeeze out excess water or spin it gently in a washing machine. Lay the sweater flat and pat out to finished measurements. Leave until completely dry. I smoothed out and slightly stretched the ribbing and rolled the front neck down a little and let it dry like that, to give the top the shaping I wanted.

Diagonal striped scarf

alpakka1053
alpakka4313
alpakka4207
alpakka5037
alpakka3031
alpakka7236
alpakka2355
alpakka7521
alpakka2652
alpakka4611
alpakka4627
alpakka4308

This scarf is one of my absolute favorites, with so many fantastic colors in one and the same garment—pure Vitamin C around the neck! It looks difficult to knit diagonally, but it isn't, and the luscious alpaca yarn makes it airy, warm, and soft.

LEVEL OF DIFFICULTY
Easy

MATERIALS
Yarn:
CYCA #3 (DK/light worsted) Sandnes Garn Alpakka (100% alpaca, 120 yd/110 m / 50 g)
Yarn Colors and Amounts:
1053, 4207, 4313, 5037, 2652, 4611, 7521, 3031, 4627, 2355, 4308, and 7236.
My scarf weighs a total of 4½ oz / 30 g.
Needles: U. S. size 6 / 4 mm

TECHNIQUES
Garter stitch: Knit all rows.

1. CO 2 sts. Knit back and forth, increasing 1 st at the beginning of every row. Increase with the "invisible" method: M1 (see page 114 in the Craft School section).
2. Each stripe is 8 rows (= 4 ridges).
3. When you reach the desired width of the scarf (mine is 6¾ in / 17 cm wide), continue increasing at the beginning of the row on one side of the scarf but also decrease 1 st on the opposite side: *Increase 1 st at beginning of row, knit to end of row; turn, k2tog at the beginning of the next row and knit to end of row. Repeat from *.
4. Knit until scarf is desired length—my scarf ended up 47¼ in / 120 cm long.
5. End with a straight edge by binding off 1 st at the beginning of every row.
6. Weave in all ends neatly on WS.
7. Soak the scarf in lukewarm water and then gently squeeze out excess water. Lay it flat, patting it out into a long even strip. Let dry completely.

EASY PONCHO

This poncho is my favorite garment! It's like going around with a warm cozy blanket all day, my own vertical tent. Perfect for me—I'm always freezing. I particularly love to wear a poncho when I have a long flight ahead of me. It can be ice-cold on airplanes, so it's nice to have a poncho around! Ponchos are also perfect for autumn, when you want to ease your way out of summer. It's so nice to have a poncho to wear instead of giving in and digging out your autumn jackets—and you can savor some of the summer holiday feeling for just a bit longer.

This is an easy poncho, knitted in a tweedy, light sock yarn that's a blend of wool, acrylic, and nylon. This combination makes the yarn easy to knit, and it'll slides smoothly on your needles. The recommended needle size is 3-3.5 mm, but I used U. S. size 10½ -11 / 7 mm to make the garment airier and less compact—plus that makes the work go so much more quickly, of course! I think this poncho would also look lovely in doubled strands of a fine alpaca yarn, but of course that would give it a totally different look. There would also be a very different drape in the poncho, because pure alpaca is a dense yarn! The instructions are for a medium-sized poncho, but you can calculate your own stitch counts for the sizing you need. I made some short, chunky tassels for my poncho, but that's a matter of taste. It'll look just as great without any tassels at all! I hope you'll feel as comfy in your new poncho as I do in mine. Comfort yourself with knitting!

In the Craft School section on page 112, you'll find a description of how to calculate the number of stitches needed for your measurements. Read it before you start knitting, and don't forget that you always need to knit a *gauge swatch* to make sure the gauge is correct. That will get you off to a great start!

LEVEL OF DIFFICULTY
Intermediate

MATERIALS
Yarn: I used a cheap sport weight yarn (CYCA #2) that is a blend of wool, acrylic, and nylon; the ball band recommended U. S. sizes 2.5-4 / 3-3.5 mm, but I went up to U. S. size 10½ -11 / 7 mm for a light and airy poncho. My poncho weighs approx. 14 oz / 400 g.

Needles: U. S. size 10½ -11 / 7 mm: 32 in / 80 cm long circular. You'll also need a long circular (U. S. size 10½ -11 / 7 mm or smaller) as a holder for some of the stitches while you knit the armholes on the other needle. A set of 5 dpn U. S. size 10½ / 6.5 mm for the neck and U. S. size 2.5 / 3 mm for the armhole edging. I used dpn; they don't need to be U.S. 2.5 / 3 mm, but I chose that size because I wanted a firm ribbing.

GAUGE
I wanted 21 in / 53 cm for half of the poncho = 41¾ in / 106 cm total in circumference. I knitted 16 sts per 4 in / 10 cm. My calculations were:
16 sts divided by 4 in = 4 sts per in x 21 in for width = 84 sts for the front + 84 sts for the back or a total of 168 sts / 16 sts divided by 10 cm = 1.6 sts per cm x 53 cm = approx. 85 sts for the front and 85 sts for the back or a total of 170

sts around, rounded down to 168 sts because k2, p2 ribbing requires a stitch count that's a multiple of 4.

1. CO 168 sts. Join, being careful not to twist cast-on row; pm for beginning of rnd. Work 3 rnds of k2, p2 ribbing.

2. Pm at each side, increase 1 st at each side (= 170 sts) and work around in stockinette for approx. 9 in / 23 cm. Next, work armholes.

3. Armholes: My armholes were placed 6 sts in from the marker on each side of the front. That means that I had 73 sts between the armholes at the front and 97 sts between the armholes at the back. Place the back of the piece on a separate circular. Work back and forth in stockinette between the armholes on the front. When you've reached the desired length for the armholes (mine were 7 in / 18 cm), place the front sts on a holder while you knit the back as for the front. Try on the poncho to make sure the armholes aren't too short. When you're satisfied with the sizing, put all the stitches on the same circular and continue knitting in the round for about 1½-2 in / 4-5 cm.

4. Now begin to shape the sides. Check the position of the side markers and follow them. Decrease 1 st on each side of each marker on every 4th rnd. This means that you're decreasing 4 stitches total on each decrease rnd. Decrease the same way a total of 6 times (= 146 sts rem). Next, decrease the same way on every 3rd rnd (=

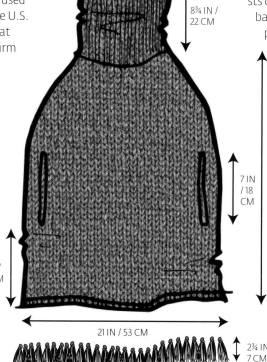

MEDIUM SIZE

10¼ IN / 26 CM

8¾ IN / 22 CM

25¼ IN / 64 CM

7 IN / 18 CM

9 IN / 23 CM

21 IN / 53 CM

2¾ IN / 7 CM

4 decreases per rnd) a total of 8 times (= 114 sts rem). Try on the poncho. If you think the neck is big enough, begin knitting the neck. If the opening is too large, continue with a few more decease rnds. I chose to have a long, wide neck for my poncho.

5. **Neck:** Change to dpn U.S. size 10½ / 6.5 mm and work around in k1, p1 ribbing for 9 in / 23 cm for a high neck, or to desired length. BO loosely in ribbing.

6. **Armhole edging:** You can skip this step if you don't want a ribbed edging around the armholes; I added ribbing to my armholes. With dpn U.S. size 2.5 / 3 mm, pick up and knit approx. 60 sts around the armhole (if you pick up too few sts, the ribbing will draw in and the armhole will be too small). Adjust the stitch count as necessary so the armhole will fit well. Divide the sts onto 4 dpn and join. Work around in k1, p1 ribbing for 3 rnds. BO loosely in ribbing. Make the edging for the other armhole the same way.

7. Weave in all ends neatly on WS. Soak the poncho in lukewarm water and then gently squeeze out excess water. Lay it flat, patting it out to finished measurements. Let dry completely.

8. **Tassels:** I used the same yarn for the tassels as for the poncho. For each tassel, cut 6 strands about 8 in / 20 cm long, and thread them into a wide-eye tapestry needle. Draw the bundle through the lower edge of the poncho. When the bundle is doubled at the center, knot the 12 ends together. Trim ends if necessary. I made 22 tassels, evenly spaced along the edge of my poncho.

EMBROIDERED WRIST WARMERS

QUICK AND EASY WRIST WARMERS KNITTED WITH GRAY YARN, SO THE EMBROIDERY WILL SHOW UP WELL. EMBROIDERING WITH HEAVY YARN IS QUITE REWARDING BECAUSE IT LOOKS SO GOOD, EVEN IF YOU AREN'T THE WORLD'S BEST EMBROIDERER. HURRAY!

LEVEL OF DIFFICULTY
Easy

MATERIALS
Yarn: Leftovers. My wrist warmers weighed 1 oz / 30 g.
Needles: U. S. size 2.5 / 3 mm: set of 5 dpn

GAUGE
Knit a gauge swatch before you start the project! My wrists are 6 in / 15 cm in circumference. To make the wrist warmers large enough to go over my hands, I knitted them with a 6¼ in / 16 cm circumference. I knitted 25 sts in 4 in / 10 cm. My calculations were: 6.25 sts per inch x 6.25 in = 39, rounded up to 40 sts / 2.5 sts per cm x 16 cm = 40 sts.

1. CO 40 sts (or whatever stitch count you need). Divide sts evenly onto 4 dpn and join. Work around in k2, p2 ribbing for 3 rnds or ⅝ in / 1.5 cm.
2. Make the wrist warmers as long as you like. Knit around in stockinette and then end with the same number of rnds of ribbing as at beginning. BO rather loosely in ribbing. My wrist warmers ended up 6 in / 15 cm long.
3. Make another wrist warmer the same way.
4. Weave in all ends neatly on WS. Soak wrist warmers in lukewarm water and then gently squeeze out excess water. Lay them flat, patting them out to finished measurements. Let dry completely.

EMBROIDERY

TRIANGLES

Before I started sewing, I drew outlines with a black pencil where I wanted the triangles to be. I worked the embroidery with satin stitch because this stitch looks almost the same on both the right and wrong sides (although maybe not quite as nice on the WS). Use a large tapestry needle with a sharp point, and choose yarn slightly heavier than the yarn used for the knitting so the triangles will fill out well. If your yarn's thinner, then just sew more stitches until the triangles are completely filled in.

DUPLICATE STITCH

It's lots of fun to embroider with duplicate stitch! For this example, I used a very heavy hand-dyed yarn to show off its color nuances. In general, I like to use heavy yarn for a stand-out effect. For how to work duplicate stitch, see page 115 in the Craft School section.

HEXAGONAL SHAWL

IT'S A LITTLE TRICKY TO KEEP ALL YOUR STITCHES PROPERLY ARRANGED ACROSS SIX NEEDLES, ESPECIALLY AT THE BEGINNING, BUT IT GETS EASIER AS YOU ADD MORE STITCHES. I KNITTED WITH DOUBLED YARNS TO MAKE THIS LOVELY SHAWL WARM AND SOFT.

LEVEL OF DIFFICULTY
Intermediate

MATERIALS
Yarn: Most the yarn used is from Sandnes Garn. I held two strands of each yarn together.
CYCA#3 (DK/light worsted) Sandnes Garn Alpakka (100% alpaca, 120 yd/110 m / 50 g): colors 7217, 6081, 4207, 3911, 7572, 9581, and 1001.
CYCA #5 (bulky) Sandnes Garn Tweed (40% alpaca, 32% rayon, 20% nylon, 8% Merino wool, 164 yd/150 m / 50 g): color 2554
CYCA #1 (fingering) Sandnes Garn Alpakka Silke (70% alpaca, 30% silk, 218 yd/100 m / 50 g): color 3021
CYCA #4 (worsted/afghan/Aran) Sandnes Garn Silk Mohair (60% mohair, 25% silk/ 15% wool, 306 yd/280 m / 50 g): colors 4332 and 3051
CYCA #3 (DK/light worsted) Sandnes Garn Smart (100% wool, 108 yd/ 99 m / 50 g):
solid colors, one skein of which I dyed in shades of green and another in eggplant and old-rose shades! Read about dyeing on page 130.
My shawl weighed 15.9 oz / 450 g.
Needles: U.S. size 10½-11 / 7 mm: 7 dpn and 32 in / 80 cm circular

TECHNIQUES
The shawl is worked around in stockinette on 6 dpn and eventually moved to a long circular.

1. With yarn held double, CO 12 sts. Divide sts onto 6 dpn (= 2 sts on each needle). Join and knit 2 rnds.
2. Increase 1 st (k1f&b) in each st = 24 sts. Knit 2 rnds.
3. Increase 1 st in 1st and last st on each needle every 3rd rnd = 12 sts increased per increase rnd. Change colors as you like.
4. When the stitches no longer fit on the dpn, change to the circular. Pm between last st on one dpn and 1st on the next so you can keep track of where to increase.
5. When you are satisfied with the size of the shawl, bind off. My shawl ended up measuring 45¾ in / 116 cm between points.
6. Weave in all ends neatly on WS.
7. Soak shawl in lukewarm water and then gently squeeze out excess water. Lay it flat, patting it out to finished measurements. Let dry completely.

DOUBLE-LAYERED QUILTED HEXAGON CUSHION

I CONSIDER THIS TYPE OF PROJECT NEVER-ENDING BECAUSE I NEVER SEEM TO FINISH, OR AT LEAST I CAN'T DECIDE WHEN IT'S DONE! I KNIT A LITTLE MORE ON IT EVERY NOW AND THEN, SO IT GROWS STEADILY, DEPENDING ON THE OVERALL SHAPING AND MY MOOD. IT'S A CHARMING PIECE AND THE HEXAGONS ARE FUN TO KNIT. A PERFECT PROJECT FOR USING UP LEFTOVER YARNS.

LEVEL OF DIFFICULTY
Intermediate

MATERIALS
Yarn: Leftover yarns—try a variety of yarn types, but make sure they're all about the same weight, so the hexagons will be the same size. If you vary the yarn types for the "patches," they'll have different looks. Blend mohair and cotton—perhaps not a practical combination, but it would be fun!
Needles: U. S. size 4 / 3.5 mm: set of 4 dpn and 32 in / 80 cm circular

TECHNIQUES
I worked all the patches in stockinette, but you can choose whatever stitches you like. For a lively look, try combinations of knit and purl stitches. You know I like mixing it up like that! The little pillows are worked around in stockinette to produce the double-layered effect; you don't need to know how to double-knit for this project.

Filling: I used a polyester filling to make the cushion soft and plump to sit on.

1. Loosely CO 20 sts.
2. Slip every other stitch to a 2nd needle.
3. Join and knit 1 rnd.
4. Now increase 1 st at the beginning and end of each dpn = 4 sts increased per rnd.
5. Knit 1 rnd.
6. Increase as in step 4 on every other rnd until there are 40 sts.
7. Knit 1 rnd. Now begin decreasing at the same rate as you increased.
8. Decrease 1 st at the beginning and 1 st at the end of each needle = 4 sts decreased on every other rnd, until 20 sts rem.
9. Knit 1 rnd.
10. Fill each hexagon with polyester fiberfill.
11. Place all the sts on a new needle by picking one st from one needle and the next from the other needle so you can close the hexagon.
12. BO and weave in yarn ends.
13. When you've knitted a little pile of hexagons, arrange them as you like and then sew them together by hand. I sewed them together with the same side facing up so the piece had an obvious right and wrong side. You can sew with a strand of knitting yarn or sewing thread.

Green and white striped
wristwarmers

Form the stripes by slipping stitches instead of working in two-color stranded knitting (which leaves floats on the wrong side). These wrist warmers are super easy!

LEVEL OF DIFFICULTY
Easy

MATERIALS
Yarn: Leftover yarns the same size (I suggest CYCA #2, sport weight).
My pair of wrist warmers weighed 1 ounce / 30 g.
Needles: U. S. size 4 / 3.5 mm: set of 5 dpn

TECHNIQUES
Stockinette worked back and forth with slipped stitches. Always slip sts as if to purl, holding yarn in back on RS and on front on WS.

1.   With Green, CO 42 sts (or as many sts as you need).
2.   Work back and forth in slip stitch pattern as follows:
Row 1, RS, Knit with White: Attach White yarn; (K1 White, sl 1 Green) across.

Row 2, WS, Purl with White: (Sl 1 Green, p1 White) across.
Row 3, Knit with Green: (Sl 1 White, k1 Green) across.
Row 4, Purl with Green: (P1 Green, sl 1 White) across.
3.   Rep Rows 1-4 = 2 rows working the White sts and slipping the Green followed by 2 rows working the Green and slipping the White sts.
4.   When the wrist warmers are desired length, finish by knitting 1 row with the cast-on color and then BO. Make another wrist warmer the same way. My wrist warmers ended up 3¼ in / 8.5 cm long.
5.   Seam each wrist warmer and then weave in all ends neatly on WS.
6.   Gently soak the wrist warmers in lukewarm water and then lightly squeeze out excess water. Lay them flat to dry.

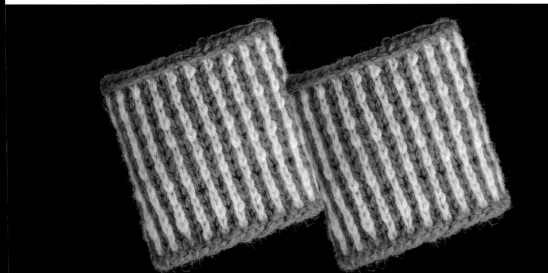

CIRCUS THROW

ONE OF MY "NEVER-ENDING" PROJECTS—THAT'S WHAT I CALL THIS LAP THROW. I JUST NEVER KNOW IF OR WHEN IT WILL BE FINISHED! I MIGHT BE VERY SATISFIED WITH THE SIZE (IT WOULD BE PERFECT FOR A STOLE) AND THEN, AFTER A WHILE, I AM TEMPTED TO CROCHET A FEW MORE CIRCLES (AND THEN IT'S A BEAUTIFUL BABY BLANKET, HURRAY) AND, WELL, MAYBE FOR AN ADULT, JUST A BIT MORE ... PERHAPS ONE FINE DAY, IT WILL BE SO BIG IT WILL COVER THE SOFA. YOU NEVER KNOW WITH THESE NEVER-ENDING THROWS!

LEVEL OF DIFFICULTY
Intermediate

MATERIALS
Yarn: Similar size (to keep the circles consistent in size) leftover yarns (I suggest CYCA #2, sport weight) in a huge variety of colors. My blanket (at the moment) weighs 1.1 lb / 500 g.
Crochet Hook: U.S. size E-4 / 3.5 mm

TECHNIQUES
Hexagons crocheted together (see page 128 for illustrations and detailed instructions).

1. **Color 1:** Ch 5 and join into a ring with 1 sl st into 1st ch.
2. Work 12 dc around ring. Join with 1 st st into 1st dc.
3. **Color 2:** (2 dc, ch 1) between each dc of previous rnd. End with 1 sl st into 1st dc.
4. **Color 3:** (3 dc, ch 1 between) each dc-group of previous rnd. End with 1 sl st into 1st dc = 12 dc groups.
5. **Color 4:** (1 sl st, ch 4) over each dc group of previous rnd. End with 1 sl st into 1st dc. Now *alternate (3 dc, ch 1, 3 dc, ch 1) in one ch loop with (3 dc, ch 1) in the next ch loop)*; rep from * to * around.

For subsequent circles, work up to last round and then join circles on the last rnd. Join into the ch sts of the next circle—see photos on page 129 in the Craft School section.
6. Weave in all ends neatly on WS.
7. Soak the blanket in lukewarm water and then gently squeeze out excess water (or lightly spin it in a washing machine or roll in an absorbent towel). Lay flat to dry, patted out to finished measurements.

Half gloves

This easy project goes quickly, and what goes quickly is also fun, right? I dyed a white yarn (Smart from Sandnes Garn) for the gloves. For the ribbing at the top, I used a regular solid-color yarn. And who says you have to make both gloves alike? Not me! If you want to try dyeing yarn, see page 130 in the Craft School section.

LEVEL OF DIFFICULTY
Intermediate

SIZE
Women's S (M)

MATERIALS
Yarn:
CYCA #3 (DK/light worsted) Sandnes Garn Smart
(100% wool, 108 yd/99 m / 50 g)
CYCA #3 (DK/light worsted) Sandnes Garn Alpakka

(100% alpaca, 120 yd/110 m / 50 g)
Yarn Colors:
Smart: 7236, 4715, 4627 + White 1001 to dye
Alpakka: 2005
One pair of half gloves weighs approx. 2 oz / 55 g
Needles: U. S. size 4 / 3.5 mm: set of 5 dpn

1. CO 38 (42) sts. Divide onto 4 dpn and join.
2. Work around in k2, p2 ribbing for 1½ (1½) in / 4 (4) cm.
3. Continue in stockinette for 2½ (2½) in / 6 (6) cm.

more is more

4. **Thumb gusset:** Knit until 1 st rem on Ndl 4. Pm and then, before working the last st, increase with M1 (pick up loop between two sts and knit into back loop; see page 114 in the Craft School section). Knit the last st on Ndl 4 and then M1 between Ndls 4 and 1; pm = 3 sts for thumb gusset. Rep the increases on every other rnd (= 2 sts increased on each increase rnd) after the 1st marker and before the 2nd marker a total of 7 (7) times.

For my half gloves, size S, the number of sts between the markers for the thumb gusset is:
After 1st inc: 3 sts
2nd increase: 5 sts
3rd increase: 7 sts
4th increase: 9 sts
5th increase: 11 sts
6th increase: 13 sts
7th increase: 15 sts

5. Place the thumb gusset sts between the markers onto a holder. If the thumb gusset isn't long enough or the sts don't fit well around the base of your thumb, do another increase rnd or two.
6. CO 1 new st over the gap (to replace the 1st st you increased around) and then knit 3 more rnds in stockinette.
7. Change yarn and work around in k2, p2 ribbing until ribbing measures 1¼ (1¼) in / 3 (3) cm or desired length.
8. **Thumb:** Place the 15 (15) sts from the holder onto dpn. Pick up and knit 3 new sts along top of thumbhole. Divide the sts onto 3 dpn. If the thumb feels too small, pick up and knit more sts. Knit 6 (6) rnds in stockinette and then BO.
9. Weave in all ends neatly on WS. Make another half glove the same way, changing colors if you like. Soak gloves in lukewarm water, and then gently squeeze out excess water. Lay them flat to dry.

Pretty striped socks

I think hand-knitted socks are so lovely, and I want to have loads of them! I also want each pair to be different. For this pair of socks, I combined Alpakka and Smart yarns from Sandnes Garn, although I primarily used Alpakka. Alpaca yarn isn't very durable, so these won't be particularly tough socks—but they'll feel plenty cozy when you're relaxing at the end of a long day.

I knitted the legs in stockinette because I like a loose cuff, but if you want your socks to stay up properly, knit them with ribbing instead. Keep in mind that different yarn weights will make the socks larger or smaller (the alpaca yarn is finer, so socks with only Alpakka will be smaller than socks knitted only with Smart). Everyone knits differently, which will also influence the sizing. Measure your feet and follow your own measurements. Don't forget to try on the socks occasionally as you knit! My socks are knitted in a medium size (U.S. size 7-8 / Euro 38) and my feet are approx. 9½ in / 24 cm long.

LEVEL OF DIFFICULTY
Intermediate

SIZES
Small (Medium, Large)

MATERIALS
Yarn:
CYCA#3 (DK/light worsted) Sandnes Garn Alpakka
(100% alpaca, 120 yd/110 m / 50 g)
CYCA #3 (DK/light worsted) Sandnes Garn Smart
(100% wool, 108 yd/99 m / 50 g)

Yarn Colors:
Alpakka: 2005, 6081, 4327, 3911, 7572, 7212, 4308,
7243, and 4207
Smart: 9544, 8264, 4715, and 2206. I also used
White Smart that I dyed in a variety of colors.
For one sock, I used only hand-dyed yarns for the
stripes, while the other sock has only purchased
yarn. If you want to try dyeing yarn, see page 130 in
the Craft School section.
My socks weighed 3.9 oz / 110 g.
Needles: U. S. size 4 / 3.5 mm: set of 5 dpn.
Stripes: Knit 4 rounds for each stripe.

1. CO 44 (52, 56) sts and divide them onto 4 dpn.
   Join, being careful not to twist cast-on sts. Pm
   for beginning of rnd.
2. Work 4 rnds of k2, p2 ribbing.
3. Change to stockinette and change colors every
   4 rnds. Knit the leg as long as you want. My
   sock legs ended up 6¼ in / 16 cm long.
4. **Heel:** The heel is worked back and forth in
   stripe pattern over the sts on Ndls 1 and 4—22
   (26, 28) sts. Leave rem sts on Ndls 2 and 3 un-
   worked until the instep while you knit the heel
   flap. Work back and forth in stockinette until
   heel flap measures approx. 2¼-2½ in /
   5.5-6 cm. Try on the socks to make sure
   the heel is not too short.

Heel Turn:
With RS facing, k12 (15, 16), k2tog, k1; turn.
With WS facing, p4 (6, 6), p2tog, p1; turn.
With RS facing, k5 (7, 7), k2tog, k1; turn.
Continue the same way, working 1 more st before
the decrease and turn until all the heel flap sts have
been worked—now you have a little heel gusset!
Pick up and knit 6 (8, 9) sts along one side of heel

flap, work across Ndls 2 and 3, pick up and knit
6 (8, 9) sts along other side of flap. Count the sts
on Ndls 1 and 4 to make sure you have the same
number on each.

5. The foot gusset is now shaped on Ndls 1 and 4.
   On Ndl 1, knit until 2 sts rem and k2tog. Work
   across Ndls 2 and 3; on Ndl 4: ssk and knit to
   end of ndl. Decrease the same way on every
   other rnd until 40 (48, 50) sts rem.
6. Now work around in stripes until the foot is
   desired length before toe shaping. Try on the
   sock. The toe is about 1½ in / 4 cm long. For my
   socks, I knitted the foot 8¼ in / 21 cm long and
   then I shaped the toe = approx. 9¾ / 25 cm total
   foot length, since my foot is about 9½ in / 24 cm
   long. Measure your foot length and follow your
   numbers!
7. **Toe Shaping:**
Ndl 1: Knit until 2 sts rem, k2tog.
Ndl 2: Ssk (or k2tog tbl) knit to end of ndl.
Ndl 3: Work as for ndl 1.
Ndl 4: Work as for ndl 2.
Decrease the same way on every other rnd 4 (4, 5)
times, and then on every rnd until 8 sts total
rem. Cut yarn and draw through rem 8 sts;
tighten. Make another sock the same way.
8. Weave in all ends neatly on WS. Soak the
   socks in lukewarm water. Gently squeeze out
   excess water. Lay socks flat on a towel and
   pat out to finished measurements. Leave until
   completely dry.

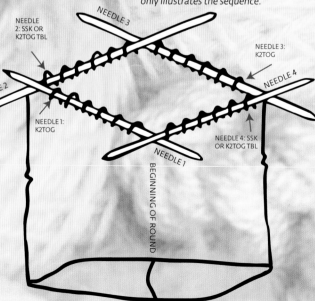

Here's how to finish the sock.
NOTE: *The drawing does not show the correct number of stitches! It only illustrates the sequence.*

SEED STITCH KNITTING

SEED STITCH (MOSS STITCH IN THE U.K.) IS BOTH A LITTLE OLD-FASHIONED AND QUITE PRETTY, I THINK. THIS EASY TECHNIQUE MAKES A RICH AND INTERESTING SURFACE—AND IT MAKES YOU FEEL ESPECIALLY CLEVER, TOO. THIS PHOTO IS ZOOMED IN TO SHOW A LOT OF DETAIL, AND IS KNITTED WITH A YARN I DYED. I USED A WHITE WOOL YARN (SMART FROM SANDNES GARN) AND DYED IT IN TONAL SHADES OF PINK, APRICOT, AND YELLOW—AND IT TURNED OUT VERY WELL, DIDN'T IT? IF YOU WANT TO MAKE SOMETHING REALLY FUN, YOU SHOULD TRY DYEING YOUR YARN; YOU CAN READ ABOUT HOW TO DO IT ON PAGE 130.

How to work seed stitch: (K1, p1) around or across. On the next rnd/row, work purl over knit and knit over purl! Nothing could be easier!

Chevron Scarf

I just simply love chevron stripes, and this is one of my favorite patterns. The chevron striping means that I can use as many colors as I like in one little garment. I knitted three long strips and sewed them together from the wrong side when finishing.

Typical me. I find all kinds of yarns in colors I fall for, and then I begin to sketch designs for all kinds of garments I want and can't find in any store. Do you also share this desire to have something truly unique—a garment that's the only one of its kind?

LEVEL OF DIFFICULTY
Intermediate

MATERIALS
Yarn: A mixture of yarns that are usually knitted on U. S. size 2.5 / 3 mm needles
Needles: U. S. size 2.5 / 3 mm

TECHNIQUES
Stockinette with increases and decreases on every other row. On the alternate (WS) rows, purl all the sts across. I worked each strip separately and then sewed them together. This shawl consists of three strips. Each strip is 3¼ in / 8 cm wide and 67 in / 170 cm long. Change colors every 4 rows.

1. CO 20 sts loosely and purl 1 row. Now begin working the Chevron pattern as follows:
   K1f&b = knit into the front and then the back loop of the same st (or try an invisible increase—see page 114 in the Craft School section)

   K7
   K2tog tbl (or SSK)
   K2tog (through front loops as for regular knit sts, but two together)
   K7
   Increase 1
   Now you've worked one chevron row.
2. Purl across the WS row.
3. Continue by repeating the 2-row pattern: Knit a chevron pattern row and then purl the next row until the scarf is desired length. On every 5th row, change colors (= every stripe has 4 rows). When you've made as many chevron strips as you want (my scarf has 3 strips), sew them together and then weave in all the ends neatly on WS.
4. Soak the scarf in lukewarm water and then gently squeeze out excess water. Lay scarf flat on a towel, patting it to finished measurements. Leave until completely dry.

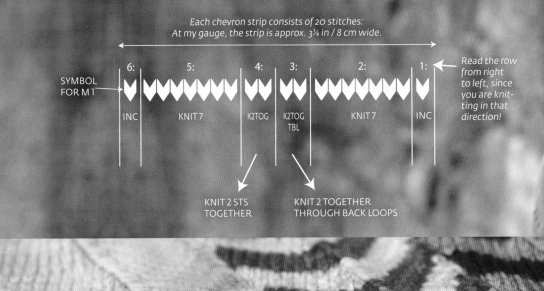

Each chevron strip consists of 20 stitches:
At my gauge, the strip is approx. 3¼ in / 8 cm wide.

SYMBOL FOR M 1

6: INC   5: KNIT 7   4: K2TOG   3: K2TOG TBL   2: KNIT 7   1: INC

Read the row from right to left, since you are knitting in that direction!

KNIT 2 STS TOGETHER

KNIT 2 TOGETHER THROUGH BACK LOOPS

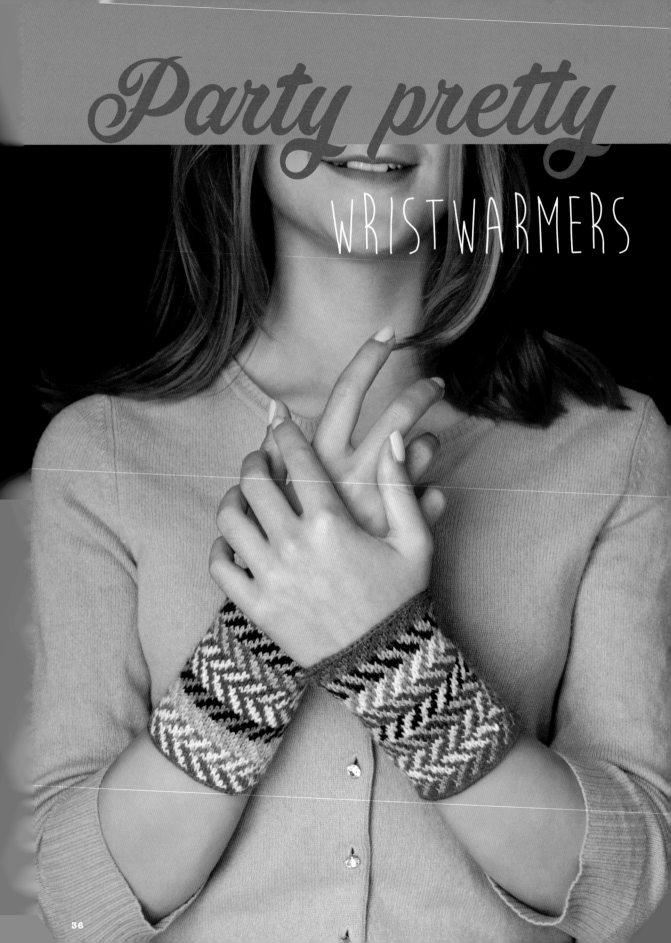

Party pretty
WRISTWARMERS

THIS IS MY NEW LOVE ... I WISH I HAD THE PATIENCE TO KNIT A WHOLE SWEATER IN THIS PATTERN AND ALL OF THESE COLORS! I CAST ON 60 STITCHES AND SOON HAD SOME WRIST WARMERS 6¼ IN / 16 CM IN CIRCUMFERENCE. IT'S IMPORTANT THAT YOU KNIT A SWATCH FIRST, SO YOU'LL KNOW HOW MANY STITCHES TO CAST ON. THE PATTERN DIDN'T WORK EVENLY INTO THE STITCH COUNT FOR ME, BUT THE ROUNDS END ON THE BACKS OF THE WRIST WARMERS, SO IT DOESN'T REALLY SHOW—AND I DON'T THINK I WOULD HAVE MINDED TOO MUCH NO MATTER WHAT!

LEVEL OF DIFFICULTY
Intermediate

MATERIALS
Yarn: I used an assortment of Sandnes yarns: CYCA #1 (fingering) Sandnes Garn Sisu (80% wool/20% polyamide, 191 yd/175 m / 50 g)
Colors: 4715, 1001, 6526, 4627, 5226, 7212, 1088, 7243, 6526, 4528, 5213
Yarn: CYCA #1 (fingering) Sandnes Garn Babyull Lanett (100% Merino wool, 191 yd/175 m / 50 g)
Colors: 4119, 2112, 1032
My pair of wrist warmers weighed .88 oz / 25 g.
Needles: U. S. size 1.5 / 2.5 mm: set of 5 dpn
Gauge: My wrists are 6 in / 15 cm around. For the wrist warmers to fit over my hands, I added ¼ in / 6 mm for a total of 6¼ in / 16 cm circumference. I knitted 38 sts per 4 in / 10 cm, so my calculations were:

38 divided by 4 = 9.5 sts per inch; 9.5 x 6.25 in = 60 sts / 38 divided by 10 = 3.8 sts per cm; 3.8 x 16 cm = 60 sts.

1. CO 60 sts (or the stitch count you need for your wrist size). Divide sts evenly onto 4 dpn and join; pm for beg of rnd. Work around in the charted pattern below. Change colors on every 5th rnd (= 4 rnds per color combination).
2. Make the wrist warmers as long as you like. Mine are 4¼ in / 11 cm long. BO.
3. Make another wrist warmer. You don't have to use the same color combinations for this one if you don't want to! Do whatever you like.
4. Weave in all ends neatly on WS.
5. Soak the wrist warmers in lukewarm water and then gently squeeze out excess water. Lay them flat to dry. I pinned my wrist warmers to a firm little pillow so they are shaped nicely.

HERE'S THE CHART FOR THE ZIGZAG PATTERN:

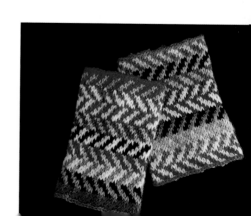

Grandmother's Blanket

LEVEL OF DIFFICULTY
Intermediate

MATERIALS
Yarn: I used an assortment of leftover yarns that were all approximately the same weight and thickness. Try to find yarns that are as similar as possible.
See page 124 in the Craft School section if you need help. You'll find step-by-step pictures and detailed instructions for how to crochet granny squares.
Crochet Hook: U. S. size E-4 / 3.5 mm

CROCHET TIPS
I weave in the ends as I go so I don't have to weave them all in when finishing. For many granny square patterns, there's only 1 chain st between each double crochet group (dc gr); but I like to work 2 chain sts between dc groups because I prefer holes that are a little more obvious. It's a matter of preference, though, so do it whichever way you like better.

Rnd 1, Color 1: Ch 5. Join into a ring with 1 sl st into last ch. Ch 3, and then work 2 dc around the ch ring (= 1st dc gr), ch 2. Make 3 more 3-dc gr with ch 2 between groups = 4 3-dc gr around the ring. End rnd with 1 sl st into 3rd ch at beg of rnd. Cut yarn and fasten off.

Rnd 2, Color 2: Attach yarn in one "corner." Ch 3 and work 2 dc (= 1st dc gr). Ch 2 between each dc gr. Work 2 3-dc gr in each corner = total of 8 dc gr around. End rnd with ch 2 and join to 3rd ch at beg of rnd with 1 sl st. Cut yarn and fasten off.

Rnd 3, Color 3: Attach yarn at one corner. Ch 3 and, in corner, work 2 dc, ch 2, 3 dc, ch 2 = 2 3-dc gr in the corner. Now work 1 3-dc gr + ch 2 in the center ch loop of previous rnd. Continue around with 2 3-dc gr in each corner and 1 3-dc gr around each ch-2

loop between corners, with ch 2 between each dc gr. End rnd with ch 2 and join to 3rd ch at beg of rnd with 1 sl st. Cut yarn and fasten off.

Rnd 4, Color 4: Work as est with 2 dc gr between each corner (instead of 1 gr as on previous rnd). End rnd with ch 2 and join to 3rd ch at beg of rnd with 1 sl st. Cut yarn and fasten off.

Crocheting the Squares Together
The following squares are joined to the previous one on the 4th rnd with Color 4. Only the 1st square is worked exactly as described above. When joining squares, work a sl st around the adjacent square's chain loops: Work 3 dc in corner, ch 1, 1 sl st around the previous square's corner ch loop, 3 dc in corner on the current square. Now the squares are joined. Continue with ch 1, 1 sl st around the previous square's ch loop, 3 dc in the current square, and so on, until the entire side is attached to the previous square. Finish the square. Cut yarn and fasten off. Make as many squares as you like—but it takes a very long time to make a large blanket, so take that into consideration.

Crocheting the Blanket Edging
Begin at a corner of the blanket. Attach yarn and ch 3, 2 dc, ch 2 and 3 dc. Now work (ch 2, 3 dc) in each ch loop around; at each corner, work 2 3-dc gr with ch 2 between each group. End with ch 2 and 1 sl st in the 3rd ch at beg of rnd. Rep the edging for as many rounds as you like.
I worked several rounds of the edging—with different colors on each round, of course!

Finishing
Weave in all ends neatly on WS. Soak blanket in lukewarm water. Gently squeeze out excess water or lightly spin in washing machine. Lay blanket flat and leave until completely dry.

BLOCK KNITTING

HERE YOU CAN SEE ONE OF MY 1,000 UNFINISHED GAUGE SWATCHES—WHICH I'M SURE I'LL MANAGE TO TURN INTO SOMETHING ONE FINE DAY! I KNITTED WITH WHITE AND YELLOW ALPACA YARN ON NEEDLES U. S. SIZE 1.5 / 2.5 MM. THE DESIGN IS SIMPLE: BEGIN WITH *1 ROW IN WHITE AND THEN 8 ROWS OF (1 WHITE, 3 YELLOW) ACROSS; REP FROM * AND END WITH 1 ROW WHITE. DON'T FORGET TO WORK LOOSELY IN TWO-COLOR STRANDED KNITTING OR IT'LL START DRAWING IN ON THE WRONG SIDE. AFTERWARDS, I CAREFULLY STEAM PRESS THE PIECE ON THE WRONG SIDE SO IT WILL BE NICE AND FLAT.

MAYBE IT WILL BE A SCARF?

boho wristwarmers

Quick-to-knit wrist warmers with a few embroidered stitches. You can knit lots of these in no time, without even realizing it ...

LEVEL OF DIFFICULTY
Easy

MATERIALS
Yarn: Leftover yarns, approx. CYCA #3-4 (DK/light worsted) for the knitting and heavier yarn for the embroidery
My pair of wrist warmers weigh 1.25 oz / 35 g
Needles: U. S. size 7 / 4.5 mm: set of 5 dpn

GAUGE
My wrists are 6 in / 15 cm around. For the wrist warmers to fit over my hands, I added ¼ in / 6 mm for a total of 6¼ in / 16 cm circumference. I knitted 20 sts in 4 in / 10 cm so the calculations were:
20 divided by 4 = 5 sts per inch; 5 x 6.25 in = 31.25, rounded to 32 sts / 20 divided by 10 = 2 sts per cm; 2 x 16 cm = 32 sts.

1. CO 32 sts and divide sts evenly onto 4 dpn. Join and pm for beg of rnd. Work around in stockinette, changing colors as you please. BO when wrist warmer is desired length. Make another wrist warmer with a whole new set of color combinations—or make them match, whichever you prefer.
2. Weave in all ends neatly on WS. Using contrasting colors so they "pop," embroider with duplicate stitch. See the Craft School section on page 115 for how to work duplicate stitch. Just give it a try—it's so much fun!
3. Soak the wrist warmers in lukewarm water. Gently squeeze out excess water and then lay wrist warmers flat to dry.

I knitted this poncho with a variety of leftover yarns in different sizes. After I finished knitting, I embroidered a few patterns with duplicate stitch. Then I added some long, uneven fringes. Very boho!

LEVEL OF DIFFICULTY
Intermediate

MATERIALS
Yarn: A mixture of leftover yarns. I used a heavier yarn at the bottom that worked out to about 14 sts in 4 in / 10 cm. Higher up, I used thinner yarns, closer to 16 sts per 4 in / 10 cm. In between, I held 2 strands together to keep the poncho at about the same thickness throughout. In the end, my poncho weighed 21 oz / 600 g.
Needles: U. S. size 10½-11 / 7 mm: 32 in / 80 cm long circular

GAUGE
The poncho is approx. 43¼ in / 110 cm in width, with the lower edge 86½ in / 220 cm in circumference. I worked at 14 sts in 4 in / 10 cm. My calculations were:
14 divided by 4 = 3.5 sts per inch. 86½ in total circumference x 3.5 sts per inch = 303 sts / 14 divided by 10 = 1.4 sts per cm. 220 cm total circumference x 1.4 sts per cm = 308 sts.
I placed 6 markers before beginning the decreases because I had divided the piece into 6 equal sections. I then adjusted the stitch count to 312 so it would be a multiple of 6 = 52 sts between each marker. Since the pattern is based on leftover yarns, you will likely use different yarns than I did. So it's very important to knit a gauge swatch to determine your gauge with the yarn you're using! Basing your calculations on your gauge swatch, measure 43¼ in / 110 cm for the width or 86½ in / 220 cm in circumference, and then determine the stitch count. Adjust up or down so the final stitch count is a multiple of 6 and then you're good to go!

BEFORE YOU BEGIN KNITTING, READ THE PATTERN FROM BEGINNING TO END. Color changes and decreases happen at the same time. See the overview in the Stripe Sequence on page 46.

1. Loosely CO 312 sts (or your calculated stitch count) with desired yarn. Join, being careful not to twist cast-on row; pm for beg of rnd. Knit around in stockinette for approx. 3½ in / 9 cm.
2. Place 6 markers with 52 sts (or your calculated per-section stitch count) between each marker. Now begin decreasing 1 st on each side of each marker with k2tog tbl before marker and k2tog after marker = 12 sts decreased. Decrease the same way on every 4th rnd 16 times total = 120 sts rem and a large opening for the neck rem. Try on the poncho to make sure it fits.
3. **Neck:** Work around in k2, p2 ribbing until neck is approx. 6¼ in / 16 cm long or desired length.
4. BO loosely in ribbing.
5. Weave in all ends neatly on WS.
6. Soak poncho in lukewarm water. Gently squeeze out excess water or lightly spin in washing machine. Lay poncho flat to dry.
7. Use duplicate stitch to embroider as you like. I used both silver and gold threads in addition to other colors. See the close-up photo on page 47. For a how-to on duplicate stitch, see page 115 in the Craft School section.
8. Cut strands 17¼ in / 44 cm long for the fringe. Thread through the lower edge of the poncho and tie. Lay poncho flat and carefully trim fringe to even up (or, if you prefer, leave the strands uneven as shown).

SO THE PONCHO WOULD BE EVEN
MORE COLORFUL, I EMBROIDERED THE
STRIPES WITH DUPLICATE STITCH IN
CONTRASTING COLORS

STRIPE SEQUENCE FOR THE PONCHO

6 in / 15 cm heathered ikat-dyed yarns of various thicknesses in beige/off-white. On the last round, I later embroidered duplicate stitch with shocking pink yarn.

1¾ in / 4.5 cm shocking pink yarn mixed with slightly darker pink on one part of the stripe for a shaded effect.

1¼ in / 3 cm narrow stripes (1 round of each color) with beige, brown, and pink.

¾ in / 2 cm pink.

⅜ in / 1 cm with dusty purple; later, I embroidered with gold yarn and pink mohair yarn.

2 in / 5 cm with heathery "potato purple." I embroidered a pattern with dark brown yarn.

1¼ in / 3 cm hand-dyed purple-pink heather yarn.

¾ in / 2 cm powder pink yarn.

1½ in / 4 cm dark brown (the same yarn used for the neck). I embroidered this stripe with silver yarn.

6¼ in / 16 cm ribbing in dark brown for the neck.

¾ in / 2 cm ribbing edged with a mixed pink and brown tonal yarn. BO with this yarn.

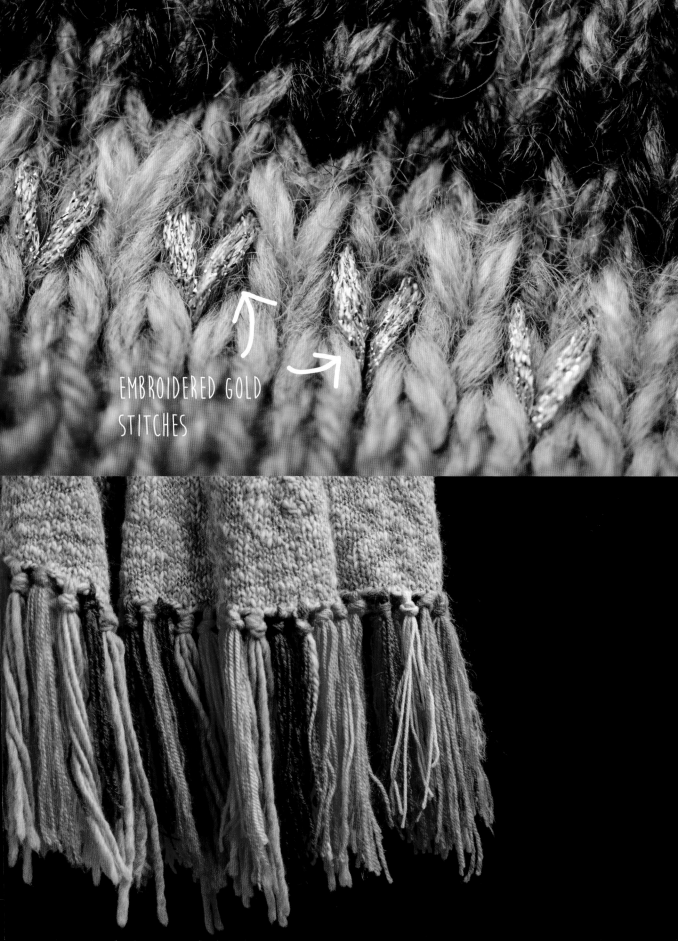

EMBROIDERED GOLD
STITCHES

CABLE-KNITTED WRISTWARMERS

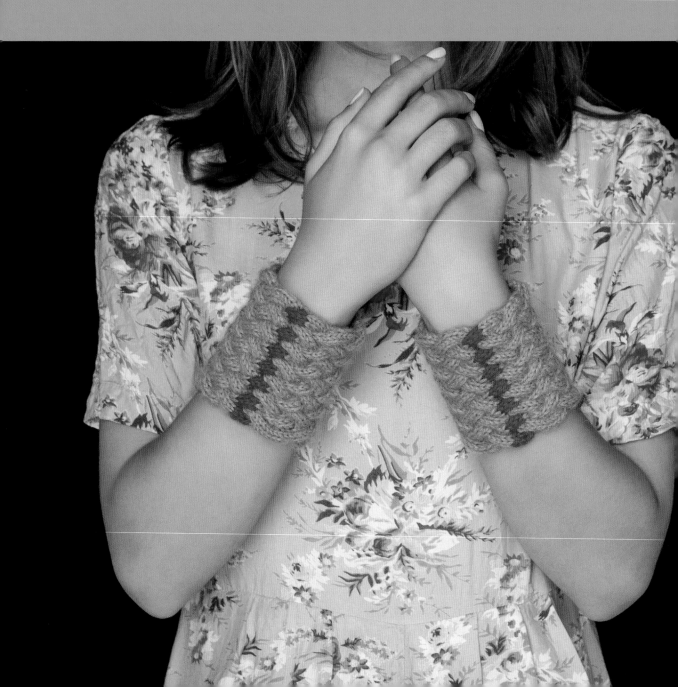

LEVEL OF DIFFICULTY
Intermediate

MATERIALS
Yarn:
CYCA #3 (DK/light worsted) Sandnes Garn Alpakka (100% alpaca, 120 yd/110 m / 50 g): 1 skein beige and small amount of pink. The wrist warmers weight approx. 1½ oz / 40 g.
Needles: U. S. size 4 / 3.5 mm + cable needle

TECHNIQUES
Stockinette stitch with cables. The wrist warmers are worked back and forth.

The cable pattern is a multiple of 6 + 3 sts + 2 edge sts. My wrist warmers ended up 7½ in / 19 cm in circumference and 3¼ in / 8.5 cm long. The number of stitches you cast on determines the length, so if you want longer wrist warmers, add more stitches. Try on the wrist warmers occasionally to make sure they fit well around your wrists.

1.   CO 36 + 3 + 2 sts = 41 sts total.
Row 1: Knit across.
Row 2: Purl across.
Row 3: K1 (edge st), *place 3 sts on cable needle and hold in front of work, k3, k3 from cable needle*; rep from * to * until 4 sts rem. End with k3 + k1 (edge st).

Row 4: Purl across.
Row 5: Knit across.
Row 6: Purl across.
Row 7: K1 (edge st), k3, *place 3 sts on cable needle and hold in back of work, k3, k3 from cable needle*; rep from * to * until 1 st rem; k1.
Row 8: Purl across.
Rep Rows 1-8.

2.   Add the pink stripe at center front: When you've reached the center of the wrist warmer—right after the 8th cable—attach pink yarn. With WS facing, p1 beige, (p3 pink, p3 beige) until 1 st rem; end p1 beige.
RS: Knit beige over beige and pink over pink.
WS: Purl beige over beige and pink over pink. Work the 9th cable with only beige.
3.   I worked a total of 17 cables, but try on the wrist warmer and work whatever you need to work to make sure it will fit you.
4.   BO. Seam the wrist warmer through the edge sts.
5.   Weave in all ends neatly on WS.
6.   Soak the wrist warmers in lukewarm water and then carefully squeeze out excess water. Lay flat to dry.

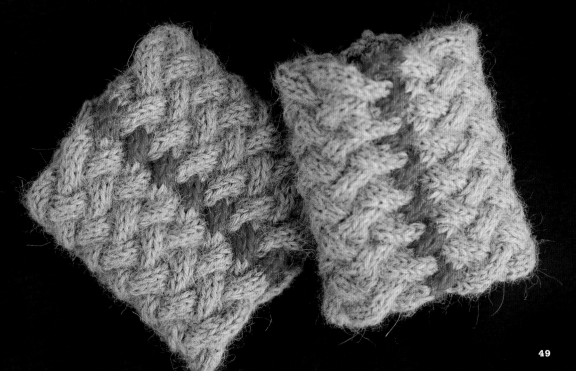

Hurray for fine tassels!

PARTY, PARTY, PARTY! I NEVER GET TIRED OF TASSELS, PENNANTS, AND POMPOMS—THEY'RE ALWAYS SO FESTIVE. I DIP-DYED MY TASSELS SO THEY'RE VERY LIGHT AT THE TOP AND GRADUALLY SHADE TO DARK AT THE BOTTOM. THE TASSELS ARE APPROX. 4¾ IN / 12 CM LONG. CHECK PAGE 119 IN THE CRAFT SCHOOL SECTION IF YOU WANT TO FIND OUT HOW TO MAKE TASSELS. HAVE FUN!

Yarn:

CYCA #3 (DK/light worsted) Sandnes Garn Smart (100% wool, 108 yd/ 99 m / 50 g): Color 1001, White (which I then hand-dyed).

Each ball of yarn makes about 11 tassels if you make them the same size as mine. See page 130 in the Craft School section for how to dye yarn before you start this project.

1. Wind the white yarn around a piece of cardboard about 5¼-5½ in / 13-14 cm long. You can decide how plump you want the tassel. Gently pull the yarn off the cardboard and wrap a strand of yarn about 1¼ in / 3 cm from the top so you have a "neck" and a "head." Weave the ends into the back of the tassel.

2. Draw a strand of yarn through the top of the head and tie tightly.

3. Cut open the bottom loops of the tassel and trim ends evenly.

4. Make as many tassels as you need for a garland.

5. Now dye the tassels. I use a little pot and mix the colors I want in it. Don't forget vinegar (or a fixative appropriate for the dye you are using) so the color remains fast. Soak all the tassels until they are thoroughly wetted before you begin—this is very important because otherwise the dyeing will be uneven. Dip as much of the lower part of each tassel as you want dyed in the dyebath. Follow the timing given on the dye packet. I begin by very quickly dipping almost the entire tassel into the pot for a light shade, and then holding about half of the tassel length in the warm dyebath to make that portion darker. When the tassels have absorbed almost all the color from the bath and the water's almost clear, I raise the tassel a little bit more so only the lowest part is still in the dyebath, for an even stronger color at the tassel's end. If you follow these instructions, your tassels will be very light at the top and gradually darken toward the bottom. Keep track of the time and temperature recommended on the packet for accurate colors!

6. Remove the tassels from the warm bath, lay them around a basin, and let them cool. Afterwards, rinse them in clean water until the vinegar smell disappears. NOTE: Be very careful that they don't felt or unravel. Let the tassels dry and then tie them onto a cord. Done!

Pompoms

WHEN I SEE THIS, I THINK ABOUT FRIDA KAHLO AND MEXICO AND FEEL DELIGHTED— ALTHOUGH YOU MIGHT CONSIDER IT A LITTLE OVER THE TOP. OF COURSE, YOU CAN ALSO SEW GRAY POMPOMS ONTO A GRAY PILLOW, FOR SOMETHING A BIT MORE RESTRAINED!

See page 118 in the Craft School section for instructions on making pompoms. I like to blend yarns and yarn sizes. When you're finished, attach the pompoms to a pillow with the thread you tied around the pompoms and sew them securely to the pillow cover. Fasten off threads securely on the WS.

Tassels for a pillow cover

I sewed this pillow cover with fabric from a kantha, a quilted camel blanket that I bought in India. You can add tassels to a ready-made pillow if you don't want to sew your own.

Close-up
of the tassel

Yarn: For every tassel, I used 2 strands of London Gold, 1 strand Alpakka Silke color 5063, 1 strand Alpakka Silke color 4554, 1 strand Babyull Lanett colors 1015 and 5042, 1 strand Sisu color 5173, and 2 strands Sisu color 3511. All the yarns are from Sandnes Garn.

1. Gather all the yarns for each tassel and wrap them around a piece of cardboard in the size you want. My tassels ended up 3½ in / 9 cm long. See page 119 in the Craft School section for instructions on making tassels. Make as many tassels as you need.

2. Draw a strong thread through the top of each tassel and then use the thread ends to sew the tassel to the pillow, placed as you like. Sew each tassel very securely, tie a strong knot, and secure ends on wrong side

GLITTERY GOLD TOP

I LOVE EVERYTHING THAT GLITTERS, AND THIS IS A SUPER EASY DESIGN, NICE ENOUGH TO WEAR TO A PARTY AND COMFORTABLE ENOUGH TO THROW ON WITH A TORN PAIR OF JEANS WHILE YOU RELAX ON THE WEEKEND! IT'S ALSO QUICK TO KNIT. THE TOP SHOWN IS KNITTED IN A SMALL SIZE.

LEVEL OF DIFFICULTY
Easy

MATERIALS
Yarn:
CYCA #0 (thread) Sandnes Garn London Gold (60% viscose, 40% polyester, 164 yd/150 m /50 g): 2 balls
CYCA #1 (fingering) Sandnes Garn Alpakka Silke (70% alpaca, 30% silk, 218 yd/100 m / 50 g): color 3021, 2 balls.
NOTE: For the reverse stockinette bottom edge, hold 2 strands of Gold together, and for the rest of the top, hold 1 strand each Gold and 1 strand Alpakka Silke together on needles U. S. size 10 / 6 mm. The shoulder straps are worked with 1 strand Gold on needles U. S. 0 / 2 mm. My top weighed 4.6 oz / 130 g (there was some yarn left over).
Needles: U. S. size 10 / 6 mm: 32 in / 80 cm long circular and 2 dpn U. S. 0 / 2 mm

GAUGE
I wanted a top 17 in / 43 cm across (= 34 in / 86 cm circumference). I knitted 18 sts in 4 in / 10 cm. My calculations were:

18 divided by 4 = 4.5 sts per inch x 34 in = 153 sts total, rounded up to 155 for convenience / 18 divided by 10 = 1.8 sts per cm x 86 cm = 154.8 sts, rounded up to 155 sts for circumference. Calculate the number of stitches you need for your size the same way.

1. With U. S. size 10 / 6 mm circular and 2 strands of London Gold held together, CO 155 sts. Join, being careful not to twist cast-on row; pm for beginning of rnd. Purl 4 rounds.
2. Cut one strand London and add 1 strand Alpakka Silke. Work back and forth in stockinette until piece measures 11 in / 28 cm or as long as you want the top to the umderarm. Divide piece for front and back and work each separately. The front and back are each worked the same way.
3. Shape armholes: BO 3 sts at each side. Next, on every 3rd row, decrease 1 st at each side until the top is desired length for the front. Mine is 6 in / 15 cm. BO.
4. Work the back as for the front.

Shoulder Straps

5. With 1 strand London and dpn U. S. size 0 / 2 mm needles, pick up and knit 5 sts where you want to place the shoulder strap. Work I-cord for approx. 13¾ in / 35 cm. (I-cord: *k5, slide sts to front of needle, pull yarn across WS; rep from *). BO and work the opposite cord the same way. Alternately, you can sew on a band or ribbon if you prefer.
6. Weave in all ends neatly on WS.
7. Soak top in lukewarm water and carefully squeeze out excess water. Lay top flat to dry, patting it out to finished measurements. Leave until completely dry.

entrelac

This accessory is either a long wrist warmer or a detached sleeve, worked in entrelac. In the pattern on the next page, each block has 5 stitches; the sleeve pictured here has 10 stitches in each block. Work it with whichever number you like!

THIS ISN'T THE RIGHT TECHNIQUE TO BEGIN WITH IF YOU HAVEN'T KNITTED BEFORE—BUT IT ISN'T ALL THAT DIFFICULT, EITHER! YOU DO HAVE TO KEEP CAREFUL TRACK OF YOUR PLACE IN THE PATTERN. I MADE A SHORT PAIR OF WRIST WARMERS, WHICH SHOULD BE A PRETTY MANAGEABLE PROJECT EVEN IF YOU FIND THE TECHNIQUE TAKES A LONG TIME TO KNIT. MY WRIST WARMERS ENDED UP APPROX. 4³/₄ IN / 12 CM LONG. YOU CAN CHOOSE ANY YARN YOU LIKE, BUT MY PERSONAL FAVORITE IS A HEATHERY YARN, PREFERABLY A DYED TONAL YARN FOR ADDING DEPTH TO THE SQUARES. I AVOID USING ALPACA YARN WHEN KNITTING ENTRELAC BECAUSE IT TENDS TO GET UNEVEN WHEN I PICK UP THE STITCHES. SO I LIKE TO USE A YARN THAT'S A LITTLE MORE "CONTROLLABLE" AND "FORGIVING"! A GOOD TIP IS TO COUNT REGULARLY TO MAKE SURE YOU HAVE THE RIGHT NUMBER OF STITCHES. THAT WAY YOU'LL NOTICE IMMEDIATELY WHEN YOU'VE MADE A MISTAKE. IN THIS PATTERN, THERE ARE 5 STITCHES FOR EACH SQUARE, BUT YOU CAN MAKE THE SQUARES AS LARGE AS YOU LIKE. YOU CAN ALSO CHANGE COLORS ON EVERY TIER, IF YOU WANT, SO THE BLOCKS ARE DIFFERENT COLORS.

The pattern for these wrist warmers is on the following page.

LEVEL OF DIFFICULTY
Advanced

MATERIALS
Yarn: Small amounts of yarn suitable for knitting with U. S. size 2.5 / 3 mm needles. I used a yarn that I think was actually designed for socks or stockings, so it is heathery. My wrist warmers weighed 1 oz / 30 g.

Needles: U. S. size 2.5 / 3 mm: straights

1. HOW TO BEGIN
CO 30 sts (a multiple of 5 sts because each block is 5 sts across). You can cast on as many stitches as you like for each block; just make sure the total stitch count is a multiple of each block count.
*WS: P1; turn.
RS: K1 and sl st back to left needle, k2; turn.
WS: Sl 1st st purlwise and purl 2nd st; turn.
RS: K3; turn.
WS: Sl 1st st purlwise, p2; turn.
RS: K4; turn.
WS: Sl 1st st purlwise, p3; turn.
Continue as est, with 1 st more on each RS row until there are 5 sts*. Now you have 5 sts on the right needle with RS facing so you can begin the next triangle as you worked the 1st one. Rep from * to * across. Now you have 6 triangles on the needle—though they might be a little crowded at the moment. Turn.

2. 1st TRIANGLE ON WRONG SIDE:
WS: Pf&b into 1st st, p2tog = 3 sts; turn.
RS: K3; turn.

WS: Pf&b, p1, p2tog; turn.
RS: K4; turn.
WS: Pf&b, p2, p2tog. Now a triangle is complete. Do not turn!

3. A WHOLE SQUARE ON THE WRONG SIDE:

WS: Pick up and purl 5 sts with the right needle (from the side of the triangle on previous tier). Place the last st picked up onto left needle and purl it together with the next st on left needle; turn.
***RS:** K5; turn.
WS: Sl 1st st, p3, p2tog (= 5 sts total); turn*.
Rep from * to * until you've bound off all 5 sts of the square on the left needle = a completed square. End with a WS row but do not turn. Begin again by picking up and purling 5 sts for the next whole square. Do the same with the last squares. The last block on this tier will not be a square but a triangle. Now you have 1 triangle and 5 squares on the tier. Here's how to work the last corner triangle:

4. THE LAST CORNER TRIANGLE ON THE WS:

WS: With the right needle, pick up and purl 5 sts from the triangle on the previous tier. Turn.
RS: K5; turn.
WS: P4, p2tog; turn.
Rep these two rows until 1 st rem. Leave st on needle and turn.

5. WHOLE SQUARE ON THE RS:

RS: Knit the st on the needle and then pick up and knit 4 sts with right needle = 5 sts. K1 from left needle and slip 1 st from right needle over it (2nd-to-last st) so you reduce the stitch count on the left needle = 5 sts; turn.
WS: P5; turn.
RS: K5 and 1 st from left needle, slip the 2nd-to-last st on right needle over it so you have 5 sts on the needle; turn.
Continue the same way until you've bound off all 5 sts in the square on left needle, then begin again with a new square (you are now on WS): *pick up and knit 5 sts, k1 from left needle and slip 1 st from right needle (2nd-to-last st) over it so you reduce the stitch count on the left needle = 5 sts; turn.
WS: P5; turn.
RS: K5 and 1 st from left needle, slip the 2nd-to-last st on right needle over it so you have 5 sts on the

needle; turn.
Continue the same way until you've bound off all 5 sts of the square on the left needle*.
Rep from * to *. This tier ends on the RS.

NOW REPEAT STEPS 2-5 UNTIL YOU HAVE THE DESIRED LENGTH ON THE PIECE.

To end the piece and work Step 6, you must now work a "round" with Steps 2-4 and then skip to Step 6.

6. BINDING OFF KNITWISE ON RS:

Work the single st and pick up and knit 4 sts = a total of 5 sts on right needle. Slip the last-picked up st to left needle and knit it tog tbl with the next st on left needle so that you decrease 1 st = 5 sts on right needle. When you k2tog, work through back loops. Turn. Purl across, ending with p2tog = 4 sts rem. Turn. Knit across, working last st from right needle with 1st st on left needle = 4 sts rem. Turn. Purl, ending with p2tog = 3 sts rem. Turn. Knit, ending with k2tog tbl with last st of right needle with 1st st on left needle = 3 sts rem. Turn. P1 and p2tog with last 2 sts = 2 sts rem. Turn. K1 and then k2tog tbl with last st on right needle and 1st st on left needle = 2 sts rem. Turn. P2tog. Now 1 st rem; pick up and knit 4 sts so you have 5 sts total. Rep these steps until the entire tier is bound off.

7. Weave in all ends neatly on WS and then seam wrist warmer. Make another wrist warmer the same way.

8. Soak wrist warmers in lukewarm water and then gently squeeze out excess water. Gently stretch pieces into shape while still wet. Lay flat to dry.

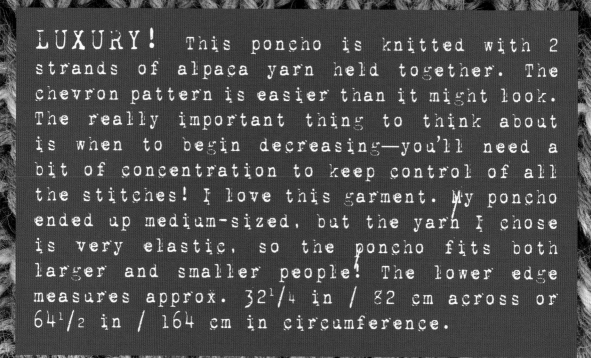

LUXURY! This poncho is knitted with 2 strands of alpaca yarn held together. The chevron pattern is easier than it might look. The really important thing to think about is when to begin decreasing—you'll need a bit of concentration to keep control of all the stitches! I love this garment. My poncho ended up medium-sized, but the yarn I chose is very elastic, so the poncho fits both larger and smaller people! The lower edge measures approx. 32¼ in / 82 cm across or 64½ in / 164 cm in circumference.

LEVEL OF DIFFICULTY
Advanced

MATERIALS
Yarn:
CYCA #3 (DK/light worsted) Sandnes Garn Alpakka (100% alpaca, 120 yd/110 m / 50 g)
Yarn Colors and Amounts:
Beige 3031: 3 balls
Mustard 2355: 2 balls
Light Gray 1042: 2 balls
1 ball each:
Light Purple 4611, Dark Gray 1053, Purple 5037, Pink 4627, Powder Pink 4313
The poncho is worked with 2 strands held together throughout; mine weighed 1.1 lb / 500 g.
Needles: U. S. size 10 / 6 mm: 32 in / 80 cm long circular

- ↗ Work with yarn held double throughout.
- ↗ Knit loosely!
- ↗ Decrease and increase on every other round; alternate rounds are knit.
- ↗ Each color stripe is 4 rounds; change colors every 5th round. Each chevron repeat measures approx. 2¾ in / 7 cm in width.
- ↗ If you want a smaller or larger poncho than mine, you must increase or decrease with a complete chevron repeat = 12 sts, or else the stitch count won't divide evenly into the pattern.

Chevron poncho

EACH CHEVRON REPEAT CONSISTS OF 12 STS, WHICH
MEASURED APPROX. 2¾ IN / 7 CM WITH MY GAUGE

SYMBOL
FOR 1
STITCH

6:    5:   4:   3:   2:   1:

READ CHART FROM RIGHT TO LEFT, SINCE
THAT'S THE DIRECTION OF KNITTING!

INC   KNIT 3   K2TOG   K2TOG   KNIT 3   INC
                                 TBL

KNIT 2 STS TOGETHER

KNIT 2 STS TOGETHER
THROUGH BACK LOOPS
(= TWISTED KNIT TOGETHER)

11 IN / 28 CM

6 IN / 15 CM

22 IN / 56 CM

32¼ IN / 82 CM EACH
FOR FRONT AND BACK

THE
SECTION
MARKED
OFF WITH
DOTTED
LINES INDI-
CATES ONE
CHEVRON
PATTERN
REPEAT

1. Loosely CO 252 sts (a multiple of 12 sts) and knit 2 rnds *loosely* (if you knit too tightly, the chevron won't form properly). Count to make sure you have the correct number of stitches.

2. Work a decrease/increase pattern round (subsequently referred to as the "chevron round") as follows: *Increase 1 st with kf&b, k3, k2tog tbl, k2tog, k3, increase 1 with k&b*; rep from * to * around. The section from * to * is one chevron pattern repeat. On the next round, only knit. Continue, alternating 1 chevron round with 1 knit round. Now you'll see the zigzags forming!

3. Continue in pattern until piece is 8 in / 20 cm long. Pm so you can space the shaping up to the shoulders.

4. Note the drawing below and pm at each point with a pink bow. The decrease lines lie between the decreases centered on the chevron rounds.

Place marker, skip 3 chevron repeats, place marker at the center of the next chevron repeat, skip 2 pattern repeats, place marker on next repeat. Continue the same way all around, alternating marker placement with three and then two pattern repeats in between—see the drawing below.

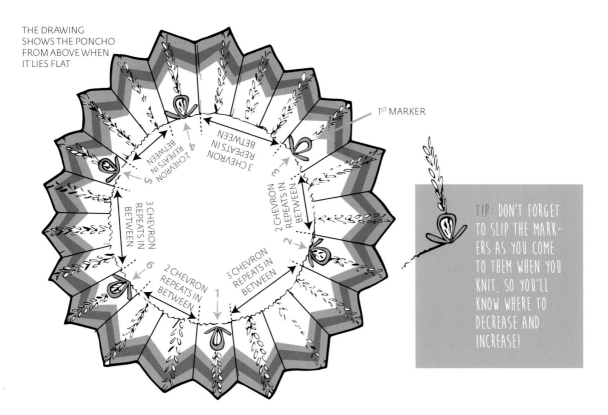

THE DRAWING SHOWS THE PONCHO FROM ABOVE WHEN IT LIES FLAT

1ST MARKER

3 CHEVRON REPEATS IN BETWEEN

2 CHEVRON REPEATS IN BETWEEN

2 CHEVRON REPEATS IN BETWEEN

3 CHEVRON REPEATS IN BETWEEN

3 CHEVRON REPEATS IN BETWEEN

2 CHEVRON REPEATS IN BETWEEN

3 CHEVRON REPEATS IN BETWEEN

TIP: DON'T FORGET TO SLIP THE MARKERS AS YOU COME TO THEM WHEN YOU KNIT, SO YOU'LL KNOW WHERE TO DECREASE AND INCREASE!

5. Decreases:
   Decrease on every 4th rnd—always decrease on the knit only round between the chevron pattern rounds. Decrease 1 st on each side of the marker = 2 sts per marker x 6 markers = 12 sts decreased on each decrease round.
   Work the decreases the same way as when you decrease for the chevron pattern = before the marker, k2tog tbl, and after the marker, k2tog.

After working 9 whole chevron stripes (Beige, Mustard, Beige, Mustard, Beige, Mustard, Beige, Light Purple, Dark Gray), change to Light Gray and begin the decreases.

1. LIGHT GRAY STRIPE:

Rnd 1: Work chevron rnd.

Rnd 2 (Decrease Rnd 1): Knit rnd with decreases; decrease the stitches marked in red in the drawing below:

HERE IS THE MARKER:

KNIT THE RED STITCHES TOGETHER

KNIT THE RED STITCHES TOGETHER

CHEVRON REPEAT

Rnd 3: Work chevron rnd after Decrease Rnd 1 as follows:

HERE IS THE MARKER:

| INC | K3 | K2TOG | K2TOG | K3 | INC | INC | K2 | K2TOG | K2TOG | K2 | INC | INC | K3 | K2TOG | K2TOG | K3 | INC |

Rnd 4: Knit around.

2. DARK GRAY STRIPE:

Rnd 1: Work chevron rnd.

Rnd 2 (Decrease Rnd 2): Knit, also working another decrease rnd: decrease the stitches marked in red in the drawing below:

HERE IS THE MARKER:

KNIT THE RED STITCHES TOGETHER

KNIT THE RED STITCHES TOGETHER

Rnd 3: Work chevron rnd after Decrease Rnd 2 as follows:

HERE IS THE MARKER:

| INC | K3 | K2TOG | K2TOG | K3 | INC | INC | K1 | K2TOG | K2TOG | K1 | INC | INC | K3 | K2TOG | K2TOG | K3 | INC |

Rnd 4: Knit around.

3. LIGHT GRAY STRIPE:

Rnd 1: Work chevron rnd.

Rnd 2 (Decrease Rnd 3): Knit, also working another decrease rnd: decrease the stitches marked in red in the drawing below:

HERE IS THE MARKER:

KNIT THE RED STITCHES TOGETHER

KNIT THE RED STITCHES TOGETHER

Rnd 3: Work chevron rnd after Decrease Rnd 3 as follows:

Rnd 4: Knit around.

4. PURPLE STRIPE:
Rnd 1: Work chevron rnd.
Rnd 2 (Decrease Rnd 4): Knit, also working another decrease rnd: decrease the stitches marked in red in the drawing below:

Rnd 3: Work chevron rnd after Decrease Rnd 4 as follows:

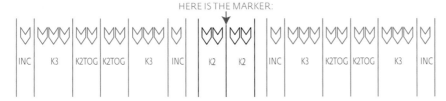

Rnd 4: Knit around.

5. LIGHT GRAY STRIPE:
Rnd 1: Work chevron rnd, but, the 2 sts on both sides of the marker are worked as 4 regular knit sts.
Rnd 2 (Decrease Rnd 5): Knit, also working another decrease rnd: decrease the stitches marked in red in the drawing below:

Rnd 3: Work chevron rnd after Decrease Rnd 5 as follows:

Rnd 4: Knit around.

6. POWDER PINK STRIPE:

Rnd 1: Work chevron rnd, but, the 1 st on both sides of the marker are worked as 2 regular knit sts.

Rnd 2 (Decrease Rnd 6): Knit, also working another decrease rnd: decrease 2 sts = 1 decrease on each side of marker. Now you are beginning to decrease from the 2nd chevron repeat because the 1st repeat has been eliminated.

Rnd 3: Work chevron rnd after Decrease Rnd 6 as follows:

Rnd 4: Knit around.

7. BEIGE STRIPE:

Rnd 1: Work chevron rnd.

Rnd 2 (Decrease Rnd 7): Knit, also working another decrease rnd as shown below.

Rnd 3: Work chevron rnd after Decrease Rnd 7 as follows:

Rnd 4: Knit around.

8. PINK STRIPE:

Rnd 1: Work chevron rnd. Don't forget that the chevron repeats with the marker have fewer stitches than the regular chevron repeats.

Rnd 2 (Decrease Rnd 8): Knit, also working another decrease rnd as shown below.

Rnd 3: Work chevron rnd after Decrease Rnd 8 as follows:

HERE IS THE MARKER:

| INC | K3 | K2TOG | K2TOG | K1 | INC | INC | K1 | K2TOG | K2TOG | K3 | INC |

Rnd 4: Knit around.

9. BEIGE STRIPE:
Rnd 1: Work chevron rnd.
Rnd 2 (Decrease Rnd 9): Knit, also working another decrease rnd as shown below.

HERE IS THE MARKER:

KNIT THE RED STITCHES TOGETHER   KNIT THE RED STITCHES TOGETHER

Rnd 3: Work chevron rnd after Decrease Rnd 9 as follows:

HERE IS THE MARKER:

| INC | K3 | K2TOG | K2TOG | INC | INC | K2TOG | K2TOG | K3 | INC |

Rnd 4: Knit around.

10. LIGHT PURPLE STRIPE:
Rnd 1: Work chevron rnd.
Rnd 2 (Decrease Rnd 10): Knit, also working another decrease rnd as shown below.

HERE IS THE MARKER:

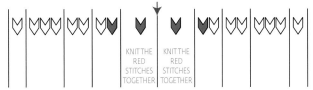

KNIT THE RED STITCHES TOGETHER   KNIT THE RED STITCHES TOGETHER

Rnd 3: Work chevron rnd after Decrease Rnd 10 as follows:

HERE IS THE MARKER:

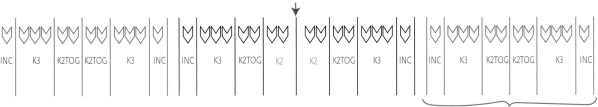

| INC | K3 | K2TOG | K2TOG | K3 | INC | INC | K3 | K2TOG | K2 | K2 | K2TOG | K3 | INC | INC | K3 | K2TOG | K2TOG | K3 | INC |

ANOTHER CHEVRON REPEAT

Rnd 4: Knit around.

11. PURPLE STRIPE:

Rnd 1: Work chevron rnd. On this rnd, just knit the 2 sts on each side of the marker—no decreases.

Rnd 2 (Decrease Rnd 11): Knit, also working another decrease rnd as shown below.

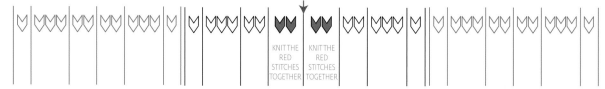

Rnd 3: Work chevron rnd after Decrease Rnd 11 as follows:

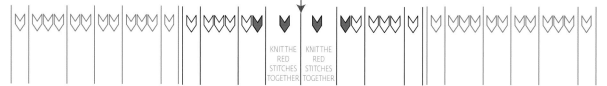

Rnd 4: Knit around.

12. POWDER PINK STRIPE:

Rnd 1: Work chevron rnd. Knit 1 on each side of marker as usual—no decrease.

Rnd 2 (Decrease Rnd 12): Knit, also working another decrease rnd as shown below.

Rnd 3: Work chevron rnd after Decrease Rnd 12 as follows:

Rnd 4: Knit around.

13. PINK STRIPE:

Rnd 1: Work chevron rnd.

Rnd 2 (Decrease Rnd 13): Knit, also working another decrease rnd as shown below.

HERE IS THE MARKER:

Rnd 3: Work chevron rnd after Decrease Rnd 13 as follows:

HERE IS THE MARKER:

INC	K3	K2TOG	K2TOG	K3	INC	INC	K2	K2TOG WITH RED STS	K2TOG WITH RED STS	K2	INC	INC	K3	K2TOG	K2TOG	K3	INC

Rnd 4: Knit around.

14. Now 96 sts rem and the neck opening is complete. Try on the poncho to make sure it's large enough. If you want a smaller neck opening, work one more decrease round. Work a chevron stripe with Light Gray without a decrease knit rnd. Use leftover yarns and work a ribbed high neck in k2, p2 ribbing to desired length. My poncho neck ended up 11 in / 28 cm wide and approx. 6 in / 15 cm long.

15. Weave in all ends neatly on WS. Soak poncho in lukewarm water. Gently squeeze out excess water by hand or lightly spin in washing machine. Lay poncho flat and pat out to finished measurements and shape at the same time. Pin out each point at the bottom edge to emphasize the chevrons. Leave until completely dry.

TRIANGULAR SHAWL

I practically live in this shawl. It's lofty and comfortable, soft and pretty! Some days I'm not quick enough, and my daughter gets to it first. I should have called dibs … The shawl is worked from the top down, which means you begin at the little point on the top neck. The increases add up quickly, and it really goes fast once you get started. You increase 4 stitches on every right side row, and don't increase at all on wrong side rows.

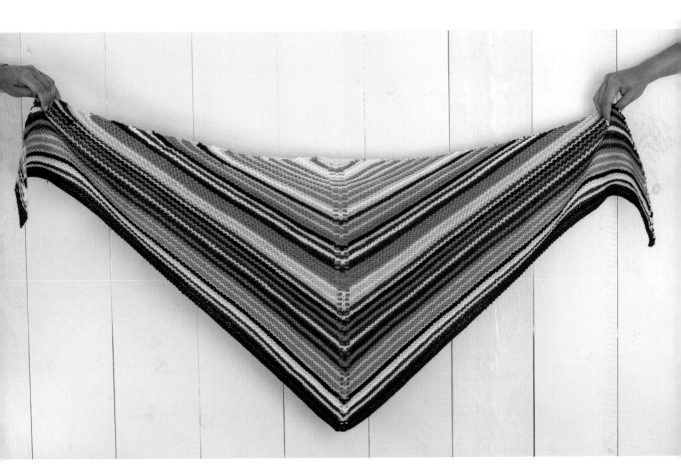

LEVEL OF DIFFICULTY
Easy

MATERIALS
Yarn:
CYCA #3 (DK/light worsted) Sandnes Garn Alpakka (100% alpaca, 120 yd/110 m / 50 g): colors 4207, 1088, 1001
CYCA #3 (DK/light worsted) Sandnes Garn Smart (100% wool, 108 yd/ 99 m / 50 g): colors 4520, 2527, 5226, 4554
CYCA #1 (fingering) Sandnes Garn Babyull Lanett (100% Merino wool, 191 yd/175 m / 50 g): 2112
My shawl weighs 9½ oz / 70 g. If you use only alpaca yarn, the shawl will be a little heavier. I combined Alpakka with the Smart and Babyull yarns so there would be more elasticity in the shawl.

Needles: U. S. size 10 / 6 mm: long circular

TECHNIQUES
Garter stitch worked back and forth.

NOTE: When working with Alpakka and Babyull yarns, hold two strands together; Smart is used as a single strand.

1. Knit all stitches! Knit these rows quite loosely.
   Row 1: CO 3 sts and knit 1 row. Pm on each side of center st.
   Row 2: Kf&b in 1st st, k1, kf&b in last st. (If you prefer, you can increase with M1 instead of kf&b—see page 114 in the Craft School section for help. Work M1 increases after 1st st and before last st).
   Row 3: Knit.
   Row 4: Kf&b in 1st st, k1, yo, k1, yo, k1, kf&b in last st.
   Row 5: Knit, working all yarnovers as knit sts.
   Row 6: Kf&b in 1st st, k3, yo, k1, yo, k3, kf&b in last st.
   Row 7: Knit.

2. Continue as est, increasing 1 st in each edge st (with kf&b in the 1st and last sts or M1 after 1st and before last st) and with a

yarnover before and after the center st = 4 sts increased on each RS row. Knit all WS rows without increasing.

3. I changed colors on every other row. Always change colors on RS rows!

4. BO when you think the shawl is big enough. My shawl ended up approx. 59 in / 150 cm long at center back.

5. Weave in all ends neatly on WS.

6. Soak shawl in lukewarm water and then gently squeeze out excess water. Lay shawl flat and pat to shape while still damp. Leave until completely dry.

Felted and embroidered pincushion

WHEN I EMBROIDER, I USUALLY BEGIN AT ONE PLACE—AND THEN SEW A LITTLE, WITHOUT HAVING ANY REAL PLAN TO SPEAK OF … AND THEN I JUST KEEP FILLING SPACE WITH STITCHES UNTIL I'M SATISFIED. THEN I SET ASIDE THE EMBROIDERY FOR A COUPLE OF DAYS, AND WHEN I TAKE IT OUT AGAIN, I'M NOT QUITE SATISFIED ANYMORE, AND END UP ADDING EVEN MORE STITCHES. AT THE BACK OF THIS BOOK IN THE CRAFT SCHOOL SECTION, YOU'LL FIND INFORMATION ABOUT HOW TO FELT AND HOW TO STITCH FRENCH KNOTS.

LEVEL OF DIFFICULTY
Intermediate

MATERIALS
Wool yarn—both heavy yarn and embroidery yarn, preferably smooth; needles suitable for the yarn, a small piece of fabric, quilt filling or carded wool for filling. Other embellishments as you like (I used a little Chinese figure that I cut off another pincushion that I had).

1. Felt the wool and let it dry. Drying can take a long time—as much as a day, so don't rush it.
2. Cut out a piece of the felt approx. 4¾ x 9¾ in / 12 x 25 cm. The naturally wavy edge can be the lower edge of the cut felt. That'll give the pincushion a dynamic look.
3. Cut out a piece of fabric to fit. Pin the felt and fabric together (see drawing on next page). I sewed the fabric on the part of the felt that was going to be the bottom of the cushion, and then embroidered the top with floral motifs.
4. Embroider any motifs you like! I started with a flower using heavy wool yarn and varied lengths of stitches, red in the center and then pink around the red. When I was satisfied with the flower, I filled in the center and the area around the flower with French knots in several colors. Design your own motifs (or study the photos and copy mine, if you like them!).
5. Fold the pincushion and sew the embroidered section to the underlying fabric section. Seam them together along one side and then fill the cushion. It should be packed quite firmly. Finish by seaming the opposite side.
6. If you like, securely attach a little figure and sew tassels at the corners. Now you're ready to stick in the pins!

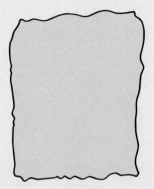

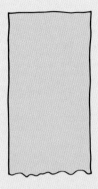

I SEWED ON THE
FABRIC HERE.

BEGIN BY FELTING THE WOOL—
SEE PAGE 115 IN THE WOOL
SCHOOL FOR HOW-TO DETAILS.

CUT A PIECE APPROX. 4³/₄ X
9³/₄ IN / 12 X 25 CM. THE WAVY
EDGE IS AT SIDES.

HOW TO FOLD THE PINCUSHION
BEFORE SEAMING AT THE BOTTOM.

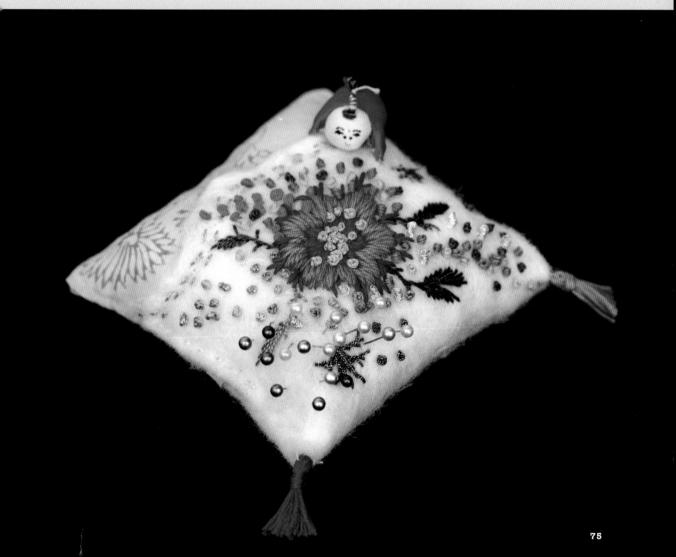

LOVELY JACKET IN SILK, MOHAIR, AND ALPACA

THIS COMBINATION OF YARNS IS THE PRETTIEST ONE I'VE EVER KNITTED WITH. IT'S SO LIGHT AND AIRY, AND THE WOOL ITSELF—SO MANY BEAUTIFUL COLORS TO CHOOSE FROM! KNIT A BACK AND THEN TWO FRONT PIECES AND SEW THEM TOGETHER. THE SEED-STITCH SHAWL COLLAR GOES AROUND THE NECK AND IS SEWN ON AFTERWARDS. FINALLY, KNIT THE SLEEVES AND ATTACH THEM—PERFECT!

LEVEL OF DIFFICULTY
Intermediate

MATERIALS
Yarn:
CYCA #3 (DK/light worsted) Sandnes Garn Alpakka (100% alpaca, 120 yd/110 m / 50 g): 6 skeins Pink 4313
CYCA #4 (worsted/afghan/Aran) Sandnes Garn Silk Mohair (60% mohair, 25% silk/ 15% wool, 306 yd/280 m / 50 g): 2 skeins Pink 3511
My cardigan weighs 14.8 oz / 420 g
NOTE: Hold 1 strand of each yarn together throughout.
Needles: U. S. size 10½-11 / 7 mm. I knitted the cardigan loosely so it would be as airy as possible.

GAUGE
14 sts = 4 in / 10 cm. BEGIN BY KNITTING A GAUGE SWATCH.
Adjust needle size to obtain correct gauge if necessary (or calculate your own stitch numbers).
Each front: 8¾ in x 3.5 sts per inch = 31 sts, rounded down to 30 / 22 cm wide x 1.4 sts per cm = 30 sts
Back: 21 in x 3.5 sts per inch = 73.5 sts, rounded up to 74 / 53 cm x 1.4 sts per cm = 74 sts
Shawl collar in seed st: 5½ in x 3.5 sts per inch = 19 sts / 14 cm x 1.4 sts per cm = 19 sts
Sleeves: 11 in x 3.5 sts per inch = 38.5, rounded up to 39 / 28 cm x 1.4 sts per cm = 39 sts

SEE THE DRAWINGS ON THE NEXT PAGE—THEY SHOW HOW I SEWED THE CARDIGAN TOGETHER!

1. **Front:** With 1 strand of each yarn held together, loosely CO 30 sts (or as many sts as needed for your size/gauge) and work back and forth in stockinette until piece is 21¾ in / 55 cm long or desired length. BO loosely. Make the other front the same way.

2. **Back:** With 1 strand of each yarn held together, loosely CO 74 sts (or as many sts as needed for your size/gauge) and work back and forth in stockinette until piece is 21¾ in / 55 cm long or desired length. BO loosely.

3. Join the shoulders and seam the sides, leaving an opening for the sleeves. My armhole depth ended up measuring 8¾ in / 22 cm.

4. **Shawl collar:** With 1 strand of each yarn held together, CO 19 sts (or as many sts as needed for your size/gauge) and work back and forth in seed st (see page 31 for stitch instructions) until collar is the same length as both front edges + the back neck. BO loosely.
5. Sew the collar around the front edges and back neck.
6. **Sleeves**: With 1 strand of each yarn together, CO 39 sts (my sleeves each ended up 11 in / 28 cm wide) and work back and forth in stockinette until sleeve is 17¼ in / 44 cm long (or twice the length of the armhole). BO loosely. Make the other sleeve the same way. Fold each sleeve lengthwise, seam, and then sew securely into armhole.
7. Weave in all ends neatly on WS.
8. Soak cardigan in lukewarm water. Gently squeeze out excess water or lightly spin in washing machine. Lay sweater flat, patting it to finished measurements while it is still damp. Leave until completely dry.

EACH PIECE IS A DIFFERENT COLOR FOR ILLUSTRATIVE PURPOSES ONLY—THIS MAKES IT EASIER FOR YOU TO SEE HOW TO JOIN THE VARIOUS PIECES. SEAM YOUR CARDIGAN AS FOLLOWS.

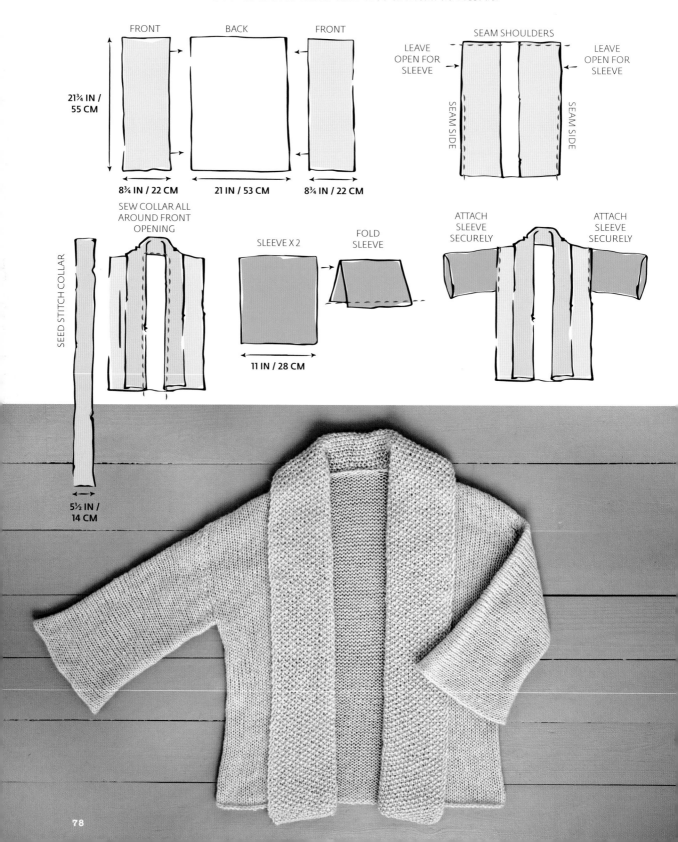

FRONT

BACK

FRONT

21¾ IN / 55 CM

8¾ IN / 22 CM

21 IN / 53 CM

8¾ IN / 22 CM

SEAM SHOULDERS

LEAVE OPEN FOR SLEEVE

LEAVE OPEN FOR SLEEVE

SEAM SIDE

SEAM SIDE

SEED STITCH COLLAR

SEW COLLAR ALL AROUND FRONT OPENING

SLEEVE X 2

FOLD SLEEVE

ATTACH SLEEVE SECURELY

ATTACH SLEEVE SECURELY

11 IN / 28 CM

5½ IN / 14 CM

CELL PHONE COZY

STRIPED COZY

LEVEL OF DIFFICULTY
Easy

Yarn: Small amounts of several colors
Needles: U. S. size 1.5 / 2.5 mm

I knitted a rectangle big enough to fit around my cell phone, folded it in half, and seamed it. I use it inside out—I often think the "wrong" sides of patterns look quite nice, and that's especially true here! Begin by knitting a gauge swatch to check your gauge. Measure your phone and then you'll know how big to make the cozy. You can calculate the stitch count by multiplying the number of stitches in 4 in / 10 cm. For example, this cozy is 6 in / 15 cm in circumference and 5¼ in / 13 cm long. My gauge was 27 sts in 4 in / 10 cm, so my calculations were: 27 sts divided by 4 in = 6.75 sts per inch x 6 in = 40.5 sts, rounded down to 40 sts / 27 sts divided

by 10 cm = 2.7 sts per cm x 15 cm = 40.5 sts, rounded down to 40 sts.

1. CO 40 sts (or the number you calculated for your cover). Work back and forth in stockinette, changing colors on every row to make the cozy as colorful as possible.
2. Make the cozy the length needed for your phone. BO and then weave in all ends on inside of cover.
3. Fold the cover and seam down one long side and across the bottom.
4. I attached a few small tassels to the lower edge. Each tassel consists of 3 short strands of yarn, tied into a knot and trimmed evenly.

PATTERN-KNIT COZY

LEVEL OF DIFFICULTY
Intermediate

Yarn: Small amounts of yarn finer than for the striped cozy.
Needles: U. S. size 1.5 / 2.5 mm: set of 5 dpn

This cover is slightly larger—7 in / 18 cm in circumference. I worked it in the round on double-pointed needles, so there are only knit stitches. It can be complicated enough to knit a two-color pattern, for me; no need to add purling into the mix! But if you prefer to work back and forth, please do. Also, the pattern motifs don't all repeat evenly into the stitch count. When I got to the end of a round, I just started the next one at the beginning of the pattern, so the motifs align vertically at the start but not the end of each round. Start by knitting a gauge swatch so you can calculate how many stitches to cast on. Don't forget that when you knit in two colors, the fabric draws in somewhat—knit loosely. My cover ended up 7 in / 18 cm in circumference and 5½ in / 14 cm long. My gauge was 30 sts in 4 in / 10 cm. 30 sts divided by 4 in = 7.5 sts per in x 7 in = 52.5 sts, rounded up to 54 for ease of repeats / 30 sts divided by 10 cm = 3 sts per cm x 18 cm = 54 sts.

1. CO 54 sts (or as many sts as you calculated for your cover); divide sts onto dpn. Join and pm for beginning of rnd. With one color, knit 1 rnd before beginning the pattern.
2. Work around in pattern following the chart. When the cover is desired length, BO; weave in all ends neatly on WS.
3. Seam the cover along the base. Done!

YOU CAN ALSO SEW A CORD AT THE TOP CORNERS AND HANG THE PHONE AROUND YOUR NECK.

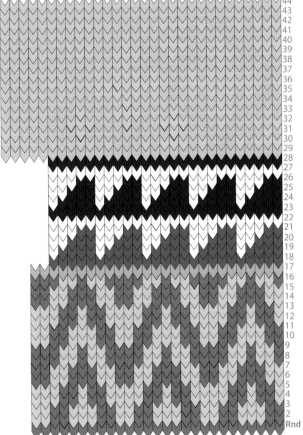

BEGIN HERE

KNITTED CABLES

IT'S SO MUCH FUN TO KNIT THESE CABLE "BRAIDS," WHICH ARE EVER-SO-USEFUL! FOR EXAMPLE, TRY THEM FOR EDGINGS ALONG THE OPENINGS OF A CARDIGAN, OR KNIT SEVERAL SHORT CABLE CORDS AND SEW THEM TOGETHER TO MAKE WRIST WARMERS. USE WHATEVER YARN YOU WANT AND NEEDLES TO SUIT THE YARN + A CABLE NEEDLE.

1. CO 15 sts.
2. Knit 1 row, purl 1 row, knit 1 row, purl 1 row (= a total of 4 rows stockinette).
3. Place the 1st 5 sts on cable needle and hold in front of work, k5 and then k5 from cable needle, k5.
4. Purl 1 row, knit 1 row, purl 1 row.
5. K5, place next 5 sts on cable needle and hold in back of work, k5, k5 from cable needle.
6. Purl 1 row, knit 1 row, purl 1 row.

Rep Steps 3–6 until cable is desired length. BO.

Simple basic mittens

It's always fun to know how to knit your own mittens. Hand-knitted mittens are cozy work, and everyone loves hand-knitted mittens as a gift. I've designed a simple mitten pattern and knitted one pair with heathery gray yarn and another pair with stripes. I used the same pattern for both, but because the heather gray alpaca yarn is finer, that pair is slightly smaller than the striped mittens I knitted with smart yarn. Don't forget that different yarn and needle sizes can make the mittens smaller or larger! People also knit at different gauges, and that will influence the sizing, too. As you knit, try on the mittens to make sure the length is right. If you have longer fingers than the pattern sizing, you just have to knit some extra rounds to make the mittens longer. Measure them and try them on!

LEVEL OF DIFFICULTY
Intermediate

SIZES
1 year (5 years, 9 years, Women's S, Women's M)

MATERIALS
Yarn:
CYCA #3 (DK/light worsted) Sandnes Garn Alpakka
(100% alpaca, 120 yd/110 m / 50 g): 1 skein Dark
Gray 1053. My mittens weighed approx. 2 oz / 55 g.
Needles: U. S. size 4 / 3.5 mm: set of 5 dpn

1. CO 26 (30, 34, 38, 42) sts. Divide sts onto dpn
    and join; pm for beginning of rnd.
2. Work around in k1, p1 ribbing for 2 (2, 2¾, 3¼, 3½)
    in / 5 (5, 7, 8, 9) cm or desired length.
3. Change to stockinette and knit 4 (4, 6, 6, 6)
    rnds.
4. **Thumb gusset:** Knit around until 1 st rem on
    Ndl 4. Pm, M1 (pick up strand between two sts
    and knit into back loop = an invisible increase;
    see page 114 in the Craft School section), knit
    last st on Ndl 4. Next, M1 between the next
    two sts (between Ndls 4 and 1); pm. Now 1 st
    has become 3! Increase on every other rnd: Knit
    to marker, sl m, M1, knit to marker, M1, sl m.
    There are two more sts between markers on
    each increase rnd. Increase a total of 4 (5, 6, 7, 7)
    times. On my mittens (which were Women's S),

I increased as follows: Sts between the markers
after each increase rnd: 1st increase: 3 sts; 2nd
increase: 5 sts; 3rd increase: 7 sts; 4th increase:
9 sts; 5th increase: 11 sts; 6th increase: 13 sts; 7th
increase: 15 sts.

5. Place the thumb gusset sts on a holder.
6. CO 1 st over the gap (because you used 1 st to
    begin the gusset) and then work around in
    stockinette until mitten is 5¼ (6¼, 8¼, 9½, 10¼)
    in / 13 (16, 21, 24, 26) cm long or desired length to
    top of little finger.
7. **Top shaping:** Begin the decreases to shape
    the top of mitten on Ndl 1: K2tog tbl (or ssk);
    knit until 2 sts rem on Ndl 2, k2tog. Ndl 3: K2tog
    tbl (or ssk); knit until 2 sts rem on Ndl 4, k2tog.
    Decrease the same way on every other rnd until
    6 (6, 6, 8, 8) sts rem. Cut yarn and draw end
    through rem sts; tighten.
8. **Thumb:** Slip the 9 (11, 13, 15, 15) held sts onto
    dpn and pick up and knit 3 sts across top of
    thumbhole. If the thumb is too tight, pick up
    more sts or increase more times in the gusset.
    Divide sts onto 3 dpn and knit around until
    thumb measures 1¼ (1½, 1¾, 2, 2½) in / 3 (4, 4.5,
    5, 6) cm or desired length to middle of thumb-
    nail. Work k2tog around until approx. 4 sts
    rem. Cut yarn and draw end through rem sts;
    tighten. Weave in all ends neatly on WS. Make
    another mitten the same way.

HOW TO FINISH THE MITTEN TOP
NOTE: THE DRAWING DOES NOT SHOW THE ACTUAL NUMBER
OF STITCHES, IT ONLY ILLUSTRATES THE STITCH POSITIONS

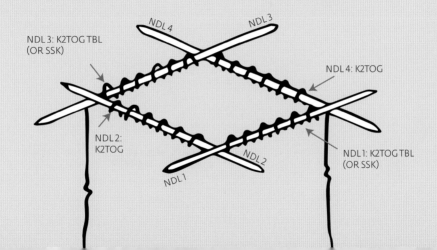

Simple basic mittens

WHEN KNITTING STRIPED MITTENS, YOU HAVE TO CONSIDER WHERE TO PLACE THE TRANSITIONS BETWEEN COLORS. I PLACED THE COLOR SHIFTS AT THE CENTER OF THE PALM. YOU ALSO HAVE TO BE CAREFUL NOT TO PULL THE YARNS TOO TIGHTLY WHEN CHANGING COLORS. IF YOU DO, THE MITTEN WON'T BE SMOOTH AND YOU CAN'T FIX IT LATER ON. SO, HOLD THE YARN LOOSELY WHEN YOU CHANGE TO A NEW COLOR.

LEVEL OF DIFFICULTY
Intermediate

SIZES
1 year (5 years, 9 years, Women's S, Women's M)

MATERIALS
Yarn:
CYCA #3 (DK/light worsted) Sandnes Garn Smart (100% wool, 108 yd/ 99 m / 50 g): 1 ball each of 1088 and 5033. My mittens weighed 2.3 oz / 65 g.
Needles: U. S. size 4 / 3.5 mm: set of 5 dpn

Ribbed cuff: Begin as for Basic Mittens. Work around in k3, p1 ribbing for 2 (2, 2¾, 3¼, 3½) in / 5 (5, 7, 8, 9) cm or desired length.

Thumb gusset: On the left mitten, increase at the end of Ndl 1 and, on the right mitten, increase for the gusset at the end of Ndl 3. (This change to the basic pattern means the color shifts will be on the palm, instead of on the back of the hand where they would be much more visible.)

HOW TO FINISH THE STRIPED MITTEN TOP
NOTE: THE DRAWING DOES NOT SHOW THE ACTUAL NUMBER
OF STITCHES; IT ONLY ILLUSTRATES THE STITCH POSITIONS

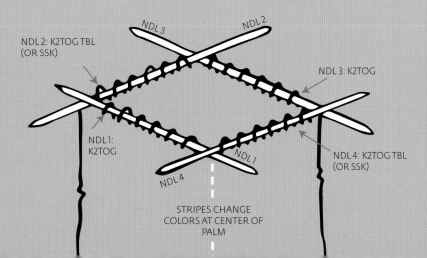

NDL 3

NDL 2

NDL 2: K2TOG TBL
(OR SSK)

NDL 3: K2TOG

NDL 1:
K2TOG

NDL 4: K2TOG TBL
(OR SSK)

NDL 1

NDL 4

STRIPES CHANGE
COLORS AT CENTER OF
PALM

I FIRST EMBROIDERED THIS CHEERY MOTIF ON A PAIR OF CHILDREN'S MITTENS! ON THE NEXT PAGE, YOU'LL FIND A CHART FOR WHAT MY FAMILY CALLS "THE SKULL PATTERN." THE PATTERN IS DRAWN FOR YOU, STITCH BY STITCH. ON PAGE 115 IN THE CRAFT SCHOOL SECTION, YOU CAN LEARN HOW TO WORK DUPLICATE STITCH EMBROIDERY. I DYED THE YARN FOR THESE MITTENS WITH BLUE AND A LITTLE GREEN. IF YOU WANT TO DYE YARN, SEE PAGE 130 IN THE CRAFT SCHOOL SECTION. I USED SMART YARN FROM SANDNES GARN.

Sizes

Sizing isn't that simple—what's normal in my family may not be the same for another family, especially when it comes to children's sizes. Children grow so differently! Do some testing and outline some hands. If you have a 4-year-old with wide hands, you might need to knit the size I've designated for 9-year-olds for that child, and just make it shorter. I tried these mittens on several children and could only conclude that hands are all kinds of sizes! I've noted the width of the hands for each size so you can see how wide the mittens are. Don't forget, though, that wool mittens can stretch a little.

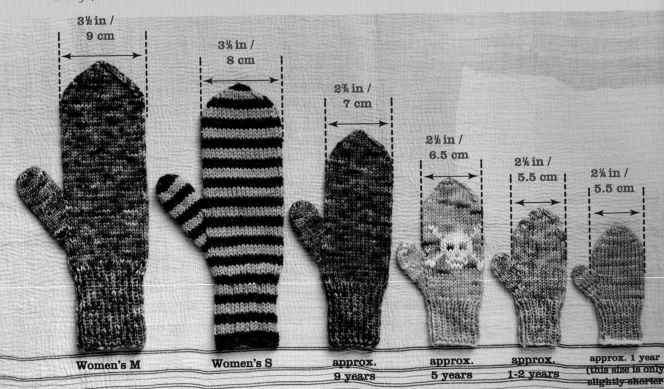

| 3½ in / 9 cm | 3¼ in / 8 cm | 2¾ in / 7 cm | 2½ in / 6.5 cm | 2¼ in / 5.5 cm | 2¼ in / 5.5 cm |

Women's M Women's S approx. 9 years approx. 5 years approx. 1-2 years approx. 1 year (this size is only slightly shorter than the one to the left!)

SKULL PATTERN

I knitted this scarf for my daughter when she was little. She really wanted a scarf with a "skull" on—she didn't know that it was called a death's head or skull-and-crossbones—and after that, we just called this motif a skull in our family! I drew the pattern (at right) for the end of the scarf. First, I knitted 5 rows in garter stitch (knit every row) and then continued in stockinette with a garter stitch edging on each side (to prevent the scarf from rolling in toward the center). To help you with the positioning, try drawing the stitches for the scarf on graph paper; that way you can center the motif accurately. For my scarf, I began with 7 sts before knitting the first white stitch of the motif and then followed the motif with 7 sts. If you have long floats on the wrong side, twist the strands around each other about every 3 sts so they don't hang loosely. When knitting a two-color stranded knitting pattern, make sure the knitting isn't too tight or the motif stitches won't show clearly. Another tip is to knit the pattern with slightly heavier yarn—that always works well for me!

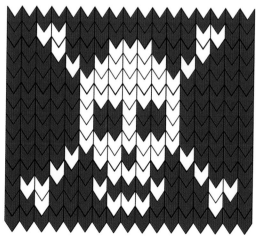

HERE'S THE CHART FOR THE SKULL-AND-CROSSBONES

more is more
BLOCK-PATTERN MITTENS

HERE'S THE CHART FOR MY BLOCKS

PATTERN KNITTING (TWO-COLOR STRANDED KNITTING) ALWAYS LOOKS SO GOOD, EVEN IF IT'S A BIT OF EXTRA WORK ... AND IT'S SO HARD TO RESIST MAKING PATTERNED MITTENS IN LOVELY COLORS. WHEN I DESIGN PATTERNS, THE MOTIFS SELDOM WORK EVENLY INTO THE STITCH COUNT. HOWEVER, I'S EASY TO MAKE SURE THE COLOR SHIFT IS CENTERED ON THE PALM—AND MORE THAN ANYTHING, I LOVE IT WHEN YOU CAN TELL A PAIR OF MITTENS WAS HAND-KNITTED. AS A BONUS, PATTERN KNITTING WITH SEVERAL COLORS MAKES THE MITTENS THICKER AND WARMER, BECAUSE OF THE EXTRA STRANDS ON THE INSIDE!

LEVEL OF DIFFICULTY
Intermediate

SIZES
1 year (5 years, 9 years, Women's S, Women's M)

MATERIALS
Yarn:
CYCA #3 (DK/light worsted) Sandnes Garn Smart (100% wool, 108 yd/ 99 m / 50 g)
CYCA #3 (DK/light worsted) Sandnes Garn Alpakka (100% alpaca, 120 yd/110 m / 50 g)
Yarn Colors and Amounts (1 ball each):
Smart: Dark Pink-Red 4600, Pink 4627, White 1001, Dark Purple 5229, Light Purple 5033, Teal 7236, and Rose Pink 4715.
Alpakka: Pale Mint 7212
My mittens weigh approx. 2.8 oz / 80 g.
Needles: U. S. size 4 / 3.5 mm: set of 5 dpn

1. With Pink 4627, CO 26 (30, 34, 38, 42) sts. Divide sts onto dpn and join; pm for beginning of rnd.
2. Knit 1 rnd, alternating Pink 4627 and White 1001. On the next rnd, begin k1, p1 ribbing for 4 rnds with Pink for the knit sts and White for the purl sts.
3. **Change colors:** Continue in ribbing but substitute Dark Pink-Red 4600 for the Pink for 4 rnds. Change back to Pink for 4 rnds and end with 4 rnds Dark Pink-Red. The ribbing on my cuffs ended up measuring 2¾ in / 7 cm.
4. **Now begin the blocks pattern:** Work 3 sts with one color and then 3 sts of another color. Each block is 4 rnds high. See the color sequence on the chart. Work 1 block, change colors, and work 2 rnds of next block before beginning the thumb gusset.
5. **Thumb gusset:** On the 7th rnd, begin the thumb gusset following the instructions for the Basic Mittens on page 87.
On the left mitten, increase for the gusset at the end of Ndl 1 so the round shifts at the center of the palm. On the right mitten, begin the gusset at the end of Ndl 3. Work the new gusset sts into a stripe rather than block pattern (see photo).
6. After completing gusset, CO 1 st over the gap so all the blocks will have 3 sts (because you "lost" 1 st for the beginning of the gusset. Continue the block pattern and colors following the chart.

7. I knitted 9 blocks in length and then alternated 1 rnd in stockinette with Dark Pink-Red 4600 and 1 rnd Pink 4627. When mitten measures 5¼ (6¼, 8¼, 9½, 10¼) in / 13 (16, 21, 24, 26) cm or desired length to top of little finger, begin shaping top. I began shaping for my mitten top at 9½ in / 24 cm.
8. **Top shaping:** See the drawing of the striped mittens on page 89 for how to set up the decreases. At the same time as shaping the top, work in stripes with Dark Pink-Red and Pink, alternating colors every rnd; work the last 3 rnds with Pink 4627 only. When 6-8 sts rem, cut yarn and draw through rem sts; tighten.
9. **Thumb:** Slip the 9 (11, 13, 15, 15) held sts onto dpn and pick up and knit 3 sts across top of thumbhole. If the thumb is too tight, pick up more sts or increase more times in the gusset. Divide sts onto 3 dpn and knit around until thumb measures 1¼ (1½, 1¾, 2, 2½) in / 3 (4, 4.5, 5, 6) cm or desired length to middle of thumbnail. Work k2tog around until approx. 4 sts rem. Cut yarn and draw end through rem sts; tighten. Weave in all ends neatly on WS. Make another mitten the same way, reversing placement of gusset as described in Step 5 above.
10. Weave in all ends neatly on WS.
11. Soak mittens in lukewarm water and then gently squeeze out excess water. Lay them flat, patting or pinning them out to finished measurements. Leave until completely dry.

KNITTING TIP

If there are several stitches between colors, a long float will form on the inside with the color not in use. You can avoid long floats by working 2 sts in Color 1, twisting the strands of Colors 1 and 2 around each other on the WS, working another 2 sts in Color 1 and then twisting the yarns on the WS again. That way, there won't be any long floating strands on the inside and Color 2 will be "locked" in place on the wrong side.

more is more
MITTENS WITH STRIPES AND CHEVRONS

LEVEL OF DIFFICULTY
Intermediate

SIZES
1 year (5 years, 9 years, Women's S, Women's M)

MATERIALS
Yarn:
A mixture of sport weight yarns to knit on U. S. size 4 / 3.5 mm needles.
My mittens weighed approx. 2.8 oz / 80 g.
Needles: U. S. size 4 / 3.5 mm: set of 5 dpn

1. With Shocking Pink, CO 26 (30, 34, 38, 42) sts. Divide sts onto dpn and join; pm for beginning of rnd.
2. Knit 1 rnd, alternating White and Shocking Pink. Continue vertical stripes in stockinette until cuff is desired length. My cuffs ended up measuring 2¾ in / 7 cm.
3. Change to Black and knit 4 rnds. Change colors and knit 4 rnd with a light yarn.
4. **Thumb gusset:** On the 9th rnd, begin increasing for the thumb gusset. Follow the basic

mitten instructions for the gusset (see page 87). *At the same time,* continue the stripes: see picture on next page. On the left mitten increase for the thumb gusset at the end of Ndl 1; this places the shift between rounds at the center of the palm. On the right mitten, increase for the gusset at the end of Ndl 3.

5. After completing gusset, CO 1 st over the gap (because you "lost" 1 st for the beginning of the gusset).
6. Continue in stockinette and begin the chevron pattern following the chart below. Work without shaping in chevron pattern.
7. I knitted 4 in / 10 cm and then began shaping the top. At that point, I also changed yarn colors and worked in alternating 1-rnd stripes in Black and White.
8. **Top shaping:** Follow Step 7 of the basic mitten pattern on page 87, but check the illustration on the next page for the arrangement of stitches and decreases
9. **Thumb:** Slip the 9 (11, 13, 15, 15) held sts onto dpn and pick up and knit 3 sts across top of thumbhole. If the thumb is too tight, pick up more sts or increase more times in the gusset. Divide sts onto 3 dpn and knit around in 4-rnd stripe pattern until thumb measures 1¼ (1½, 1¾, 2, 2½) in / 3 (4, 4.5, 5, 6) cm or desired length to middle of thumbnail. Work k2tog around until approx. 4 sts rem. Cut yarn and draw end through rem sts; tighten. Weave in all ends

HERE'S THE CHART FOR THE CHEVRON PATTERN

neatly on WS. Make another mitten the same way, reversing placement of gusset as described in Step 4 above.

10. Weave in all ends neatly on WS.
11. Soak mittens in lukewarm water and then gently squeeze out excess water. Lay them flat, patting or pinning them out to finished measurements. Leave until completely dry.

HOW TO FINISH THE STRIPES AND CHEVRON MITTEN TOP

NOTE: THE DRAWING ONLY ILLUSTRATES THE STITCH POSITIONS AND DOES NOT SHOW THE ACTUAL NUMBER OF STITCHES.

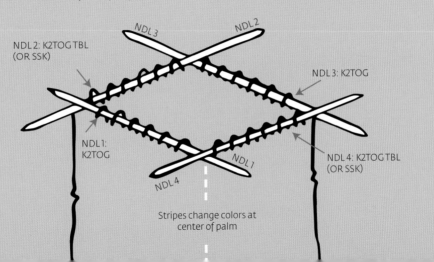

NDL 3

NDL 2

NDL 2: K2TOG TBL (OR SSK)

NDL 3: K2TOG

NDL 1: K2TOG

NDL 1

NDL 4

NDL 4: K2TOG TBL (OR SSK)

Stripes change colors at center of palm

Classic Baby Hat

STRIPED, CLASSIC BABY HAT KNITTED IN SOFT, PRETTY BABY WOOL. I KNITTED STRIPES WITH 2 ROWS OF EACH COLOR SO THE HAT WOULD HAVE A RIGHT AND A WRONG SIDE. LIGHT PURPLE AND POWDER PINK IN THE OPENING STRIPE SECTION, DARK PURPLE AND TURQUOISE IN THE NEXT, AND THEN OFF-WHITE AND LIGHT PURPLE FOR THE FOLLOWING TWO SECTIONS, DARK PURPLE AND TURQUOISE FOR THE NEXT—AND LIGHT PURPLE AND POWDER PINK FOR THE FINAL PART.

LEVEL OF DIFFICULTY
Easy

SIZE
Approx. 6 months.

MATERIALS
Yarn:
CYCA #1 (fingering) Sandnes Garn Babyull Lanett (100% Merino wool, 191 yd/175 m / 50 g): 1015, 5213, 7212, 3511, and 5042. My hat weighed 1.4 oz / 40 g.
Needles: U. S. size 2.5 / 3 mm

TECHNIQUES
Garter stitch worked back and forth. The hat is knitted in several sections, as you can see in the photo on page 99. Always increase and decrease 2 sts inside each edge st for a nice edge. All the increases are worked invisibly with M1 (see page 114 in the Craft School section for instructions).

1. **Section 1:**
   In the 1st section, 2 sts inside the edge st at each side, decrease 1 st at the beginning of the row and increase 1 st at the end of the row on every other row; alternate rows are knitted across. CO 40 sts and knit 1 row = RS. On next row, 2 sts inside the edge st at each side, decrease 1 st at the beginning of the row and increase 1 st at the end of the row. Knit next row. Change colors on every other row (= every RS row). Continue increasing and decreasing in stripe pattern 20 times total = 40 rows.

2. **Section 2:**
   Now, *2 sts inside the edge st at each side, increase 1 st at the beginning of the row and decrease 1 st at the end of the row on every other row. Knit every WS row. Work from * a total of 20 times = 40 rows.

3. **Section 3:**
   On next row, *2 sts inside the edge st at each side, decrease 1 st at the beginning of the row and increase 1 st at the end of the row. Knit every WS row. Work from * a total of 10 times = 20 rows.

4. **Section 4:**
   On RS, *2 sts inside the edge st at each side, increase 1 st at the beginning of the row and decrease 1 st at the end of the row on every other row. Knit every WS row. Work from * a total of 10 times = 20 rows.

5. **Section 5:**
   On RS, *2 sts inside the edge st at each side, decrease 1 st at the beginning of the row and increase 1 st at the end of the row. Knit every WS row. Work from * a total of 20 times = 40 rows.

6. **Section 6:**
   On RS, *2 sts inside the edge st at each side, increase 1 st at the beginning of the row and decrease 1 st at the end of the row on every other row. Knit every WS row. Work from * a total of 20 times = 40 rows.

7. BO and weave in all ends neatly on WS.

8. Knit 2 cords (or sew on ribbons). I cast on 5 sts and knitted around in stockinette for approx. 9 in / 23 cm. BO and make another cord the same way. Alternatively, knit I-cords: *k5, slide sts to front of needle, pull yarn across WS; rep from *. Attach the cords at the points of the hat—see photo.

9. Seam the hat by placing the cast-on edge against the bound-off edge and sew together as invisibly as possible. Place the points together and sew the hat at the top to form a star.

10. Soak the hat lightly in lukewarm water and then gently squeeze out excess water. Lay flat to dry.

* CHANGE COLORS ON EVERY OTHER ROW = EVERY RS ROW
* DECREASE/INCREASE ON EVERY OTHER ROW = EVERY RS ROW
* DECREASE AND INCREASE 2 STITCHES INSIDE THE EDGE STS.

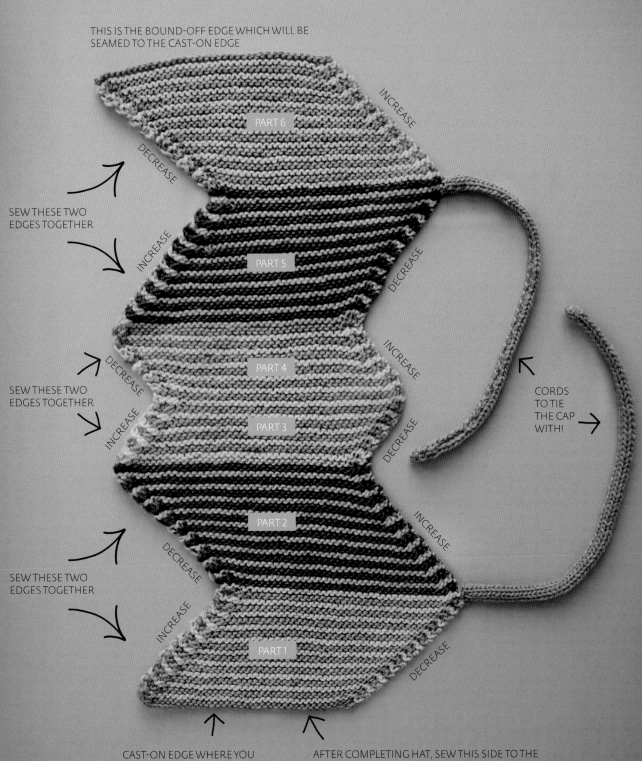

THIS IS THE BOUND-OFF EDGE WHICH WILL BE
SEAMED TO THE CAST-ON EDGE

INCREASE

DECREASE

SEW THESE TWO
EDGES TOGETHER

INCREASE

PART 6

PART 5

DECREASE

DECREASE

SEW THESE TWO
EDGES TOGETHER

INCREASE

PART 4

INCREASE

PART 3

DECREASE

SEW THESE TWO
EDGES TOGETHER

DECREASE

PART 2

INCREASE

INCREASE

PART 1

DECREASE

CORDS
TO TIE
THE CAP
WITH!

CAST-ON EDGE WHERE YOU
BEGAN KNITTING

AFTER COMPLETING HAT, SEW THIS SIDE TO THE
OPPOSITE SIDE (BOUND-OFF EDGE)

TRIANGULAR SCARF FOR LITTLE ONES

THIS MULTI-STRIPED TRIANGULAR SCARF IS SOFT AND PRETTY, ESPECIALLY WITH THREE PLUMP POMPOMS. THIS SCARF IS KNITTED FROM THE TOP DOWN, WHICH MEANS THAT IT BEGINS WITH JUST A FEW STITCHES AT THE NECK AND INCREASES QUICKLY, SO YOU'LL BE OFF TO A FAST START! IT'S SHAPED WITH 4 INCREASES ON EACH RIGHT-SIDE ROW; THE WRONG-SIDE ROWS ARE KNITTED WITHOUT ANY INCREASES. ALWAYS INCREASE THE SAME WAY, WITH 1 STITCH IN EACH EDGE STITCH AND 2 STITCHES AT THE CENTER STITCH. THE SCARF IS SIZED FOR A CHILD, BUT OF COURSE YOU CAN CONTINUE KNITTING AND INCREASING TO WHATEVER SIZE YOU WANT. YOU CAN TIE THE SCARF AT THE TIPS WITH THE POMPOMS UNDER YOUR CHIN—LIKE A COWGIRL!

LEVEL OF DIFFICULTY
Easy

MATERIALS
Yarn:
CYCA #1 (fingering) Sandnes Garn Babyull Lanett (100% Merino wool, 191 yd/175 m / 50 g): 1015, 5213, 7212, 3511, 5042.
My scarf weighed 1¼ oz / 35 g.
Needles: U. S. size 1.5 / 2.5 mm: long circular

TECHNIQUES
Garter stitch = knit all rows. Knit the first few rows loosely.

1. CO 3 sts.
2. Knit 1 row; pm around center st.
   Row 2 (RS): Kf&b into 1st st, k1, kf&b into last st = 5 sts. Alternatively, you can increase with M1 (see page 114 in the Craft School section for instructions).
   Row 3: Knit.
   Row 4: Kf&b in 1st st, k1, yo, k1 (center st), yo, k1, kf&b.

Row 5: Knit across, including all yarnovers.
Row 6: Kf&b in 1st st, k3, yo, k1 (center st), yo, k3, kf&b.
Row 7: Knit across.
Continue increasing as est on all RS rows = 4 sts increased on each RS row. Knit all WS rows without any increases.

3. I chose to change colors on every other row. Make sure you always change colors on RS rows.
4. When you think the scarf is big enough, BO loosely. My scarf ended up approx. 17¾ in / 45 cm long.
5. Weave in all ends neatly on WS.
6. Soak scarf lightly in lukewarm water. Gently squeeze out excess water. Lay flat to dry, patting or pinning to finished measurements while still damp. Leave until completely dry.

Pompoms: See page 118 in the Craft School section for instructions. **NOTE:** Keep in mind that babies like to stuff things in their mouths—if you're making this scarf for a young child, attach the pompoms very securely or omit them altogether.

TRIANGULAR COVERLET FOR THE LITTLEST

MORE IS MORE! THIS COVERLET IS ABOUT AS FAR AS YOU CAN GET FROM A MASS-PRODUCED BLANKET. IT'S ONLY WHEN YOU KNIT A PROJECT YOURSELF THAT YOU CAN COMBINE SO MANY PRETTY COLORS—ALMOST 40, IN THIS CASE. IT'S ESPECIALLY GREAT IF YOU HAVE A LOT OF PRETTY LEFTOVER YARNS. BECAUSE LEFTOVER YARNS MAY BE DIFFERENT WEIGHTS, THE TRIANGLES MIGHT BE SOMEWHAT UNEVEN WHEN YOU SEW THEM TOGETHER, BUT ALL YOU NEED TO DO IS STEAM PRESS THE BLANKET ON THE WRONG SIDE, AND VOILA! SUDDENLY IT'LL BE SMOOTH AND PRETTY. IF YOU CAN, THOUGH, IT'S BEST TO SELECT YARNS AS CLOSE IN WEIGHT AND THICKNESS AS POSSIBLE. I KNITTED TWO ROWS OF EACH COLOR FOR THE STRIPED TRIANGLES.

LEVEL OF DIFFICULTY
Intermediate

MATERIALS
Yarn: Leftover yarns of similar weights. My blanket weighed 7¼ oz / 205 g (before finishing the back with a fabric lining).
Notions: Cotton jersey fabric at least 1¼ in / 3 cm larger on all sides than coverlet.
Needles: U. S. size 4 / 3.5 mm

TECHNIQUES
Stockinette st worked back and forth.

1. CO 3 sts. Purl 1 row; turn. Now knit 1 row, increasing 1 st in each edge st with kf&b. Each RS (knit) row begins and ends with an increase, but WS (purl) rows are worked without any increases. Continue shaping until there are 31 sts on the needle. Purl last row on WS and then BO knitwise on RS.
2. Make as many triangles as you need/want. Sew the triangles together. I used sewing thread with the WS facing and tried to make sure the stitches didn't show on the RS. I like invisible seams!
3. Make half triangles for the sides so the blanket will be a straight-edged rectangle. CO 3 sts, purl 1 row; turn. Increase only on one side so it will be larger; keep the opposite edge straight. I knitted until there were around 16 sts on the needle, but the number depended on whether I used a fine or heavy yarn. Lay the half triangle on the blanket to make sure it fits. BO and attach to blanket.
4. After sewing all the triangles together, very gently steam press the blanket on the wrong side—use a lot of steam but low heat.
5. **Backing:** I lined my coverlet with a jersey fabric that's stretchy and very soft. Cut the fabric so it extends approx. 1¼ in / 3 cm past the coverlet on all edges. Fold in the edges and pin lining to coverlet. Sew down by hand or machine; I prefer hand-seaming.
6. Wash the coverlet by hand and lay flat to dry.

THE COVERLET LINING IN COTTON JERSEY

EASY BABY VEST

HERE'S A SMALL, QUICK-TO-KNIT VEST. YOU CAN EMBELLISH IT WITH AS MANY FLOWERS AS YOU LIKE. I KNITTED IT WITH LEFTOVER COTTON YARN SO IT WOULD BE SOFT AGAINST THE BODY. IT'S DESIGNED TO FIT A 6- TO 12-MONTH-OLD LITTLE SWEETIE.

FLOWERS AND LEAVES:

The flowers are crocheted with regular cotton yarn and hook U. S. size D-3 / 3 mm. Ch 5 and join into a ring with 1 sl st into 1st ch. Work sc around the ring until well filled. Ch 4 + 1 sl st around the ring to make several chain loops. Make 4 ch loops (or as many as you want to have or have space for). Work sc around each ch loop so the flower petals will be thick (see photo).

Crochet the leaves with embroidery thread and a steel hook size 1 / 2.25 mm: Ch 8, turn and, along foundation row, work 1 sl st, 1 sc, 1 hdc, 1 dc, 1 hdc, 1 sc, 1 sl st. Work the same way along the other side of foundation chain. Cut yarn and fasten off.

BUTTON LOOPS AT THE SHOULDERS CROCHETED WITH YELLOW EMBROIDERY THREAD

LEVEL OF DIFFICULTY
Intermediate

MATERIALS
Yarn: Leftover cotton yarn. I selected a strong yellow and light pink for this vest. For the flowers, I used regular cotton yarn in many colors; for the leaves, I used fine embroidery thread. My finished vest weighed 2½ oz / 70 g.

Notions: 2 buttons.

Needles: U. S. size 6 / 4 mm

Crochet Hook: U. S. size D-3 / 3 mm for the plump flowers and steel hook size 1 / 2.25 mm for the embroidery thread, used for the leaves.

GAUGE
My measurements for this vest ended up at 10¾ in / 27 cm across, 21¼ in / 54 cm in circumference. I knitted 22 sts in 4 in / 10 cm, so my calculations were as follows: 5.5 sts per inch x 10¾ in = 59.1 sts for the back, rounded up to 60 sts / 2.2 sts per cm x 27 = 59.4 sts for the back, rounded up to 60 sts. I used 60 sts for the front to match the back. Do you want a vest in another size? Measure the child around the stomach, and then add a couple inches / a few centimeters so the vest won't be too tight. Knit a gauge swatch and then calculate the number of stitches you need: sts per inch / per cm x measurement of stomach = number of stitches. Adjust needle size to obtain correct gauge if necessary (or calculate your own stitch numbers).

1. **Back:** With Yellow, CO as many stitches as you need (in my case, 60 sts). Purl 1 row (RS), knit 1 row, purl 1 row, knit 1 row for reverse stockinette at the lower edge.

2. Change to Pink and stockinette. The RS is now knit sts. Work 4 rows in stockinette.

3. Alternate working 4 rows each Yellow and Pink until vest measures approx. 8¼ in / 21 cm (child's torso length up to underarm). Shape armhole on every other row: BO 3 sts at each side, work 1 row, BO 1 st at each side, work 1 row, BO 1 st at each side.

4. Continue in stockinette and stripes as est until armhole is desired depth. For my vest, the armhole depth ended up 5¼ in / 13 cm from the 1st decrease at underarm. BO loosely. Weave in all ends neatly on WS.

5. Make the front as for the back.

6. Lightly steam press the pieces on WS under a damp pressing cloth.

7. Seam one shoulder. Sew two buttons onto the front at the open shoulder. On back shoulder, crochet 2 button loops to fit buttons. I crocheted with fine embroidery thread and steel hook size 1 (2.25 mm). Make sure the loops are very securely attached so they won't fall off as the vest is worn. Seam sides.

8. Crochet the flowers and leaves and sew them on securely, spaced randomly across the top of the front. See photos.

9. Soak the vest in lukewarm water and then gently squeeze out excess water. Lay vest flat and pat out to finished measurements while it is still damp. I rolled down the front neck to form a loose bowed shape. Leave until completely dry.

TIP: FOR A PRETTY CLOTHES HANGER, CUT OR TEAR A PIECE OF FINE FABRIC IN STRIPS APPROX. ¾ IN / 2 CM WIDE. WIND THE STRIPS AROUND A REGULAR CLOTHES HANGER AND SECURE WITH A DROP OR TWO OF FABRIC GLUE. VOILA!

SWEET CHILDREN'S SWEATER
WITH STRIPES AND GLITTER

I TOTALLY FELL IN LOVE WITH THESE COLORS: POWDER PINK, PURPLE, AND TURQUOISE, ALL COMBINED. … PLUS A LITTLE SILVER GLITTER ADDED IN. JUST PERFECT! THE SWEATER IS ABOUT 24 IN / 61 CM AROUND THE STOMACH AND IS SIZED FOR A SMALL PERSON ABOUT 1-2 YEARS OLD. DON'T FORGET TO KNIT A GAUGE SWATCH FIRST SO YOU'LL HAVE THE RIGHT MEASUREMENTS FROM THE GET-GO. THE SWEATER IS WORKED IN STOCKINETTE STITCH EXCEPT FOR THE EDGES.

LEVEL OF DIFFICULTY
Advanced

MATERIALS
Yarn:
CYCA #1 (fingering) Sandnes Garn Sisu (80% wool/20% polyamide, 191 yd/175 m / 50 g): 1 ball each of 5173, 3511, 7212, 5213, 6526, and 7243 (see photo of colors on page 109)
CYCA #0 (thread) Sandnes Garn London Silver (60% viscose, 40% polyester, 164 yd/150 m /50 g): 2 balls. Hold 2 strands of London together throughout. My sweater weighed 4.6 oz / 130 g. There will be leftover yarn.
Needles: U. S. 2.5 / 3 mm: 24 and 32 in / 60 and 80 cm long circulars and set of 5 dpn. I used the longer circular when knitting rounds of raglan shaping. When the stitches are tight around the needle as when knitting the sleeves, I use the long circular as a "magic loop" to make it easier. Read more about magic loop knitting on page 113 in the Craft School section. For the neck and sleeves, use dpn.

GAUGE
The sweater should be approx. 24 in / 61 cm in circumference around the stomach. I knitted 29 sts in 4 in / 10 cm, so my calculations were as follows: 29 sts divided by 4 in = 7.25 sts per inch x 24 in = 174 sts, rounded up to 176 for ease of raglan calculations / 29 sts divided by 10 cm = 2.9 sts per cm x 61 cm = 176 sts for the circumference. The sleeves should be 6¾ in / 17 cm in circumference, which came out to 7.25 sts per inch x 6.75 in = 49 sts / 2.9 sts per cm x 17 cm = 49 sts.
Adjust needle size to obtain correct gauge if necessary (or calculate your own stitch numbers).

1. **Body:** With shorter circular U. S. size 2.5 / 3 mm and Purple 5226 (or any other color you like),

CO 176 sts (or the stitch count you calculated). Join, being careful not to twist cast-on row. Pm for beginning of rnd. Purl 4 rnds and then knit 3 rnds the same color. Change colors every 8th rnd so each stripe has 7 rnds in stockinette. When knitting with the silver thread, hold 2 strands together. Work straight up.

2. When piece measures approx. 8¾ in / 22 cm long, try the sweater on the child to make sure it's long enough. **NOTE:** Begin raglan shaping after completing a stripe. Count out to the side st at each side and pm around each side st. BO 3 sts at each side of each marker = 6 sts decreased at each side = 12 sts decrease per rnd. (On my sweater with 176 sts—half of 176 = 88 sts for the front and 88 sts for the back. BO 6 sts at each side = 82 sts rem each for front and back.)

3. **Sleeves (make both alike):** With dpn and the same color as for the lower edge of the body, CO 49 sts. Divide sts onto dpn and join. Purl 4 rnds and then knit 3 rnds. Continue in stockinette and stripes as for body. When sleeve measures 1½ in / 4 cm, increase 2 sts centered at underarm = increase 1 st before and 1 st after the center underarm st. Also, change colors at the center underarm st. For how to make invisible increases, see page 114 in the Craft School section. Increase the same way every 1¼ in / 3 cm a total of 7 times = 63 sts. Continue without further shaping to the last stripe to match stripe on body before shaping the armhole. My sleeves ended up measuring approx. 8¾ in / 22 cm up to the armhole. Measure the child to make sure the sleeves are the right length.

4. When knitting the last rnd of the last stripe, BO 6 sts centered at the underarm. These bound-off sts will later be joined to those on the underarm of the body.

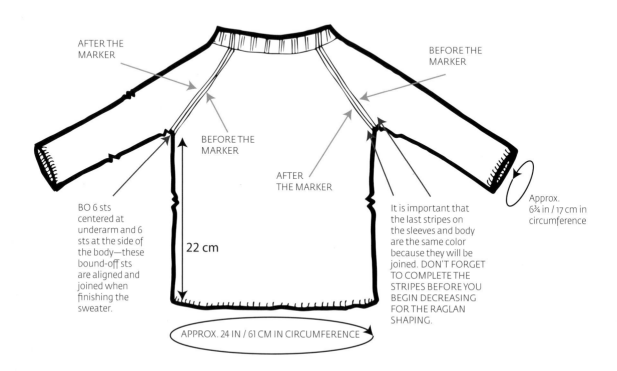

RAGLAN SHAPING
BEFORE THE MARKER: K2TOG, K1
AFTER THE MARKER: K1, SSK

AFTER THE MARKER

BEFORE THE MARKER

BEFORE THE MARKER

AFTER THE MARKER

BO 6 sts centered at underarm and 6 sts at the side of the body—these bound-off sts are aligned and joined when finishing the sweater.

It is important that the last stripes on the sleeves and body are the same color because they will be joined. DON'T FORGET TO COMPLETE THE STRIPES BEFORE YOU BEGIN DECREASING FOR THE RAGLAN SHAPING.

Approx. 6¾ in / 17 cm in circumference

22 cm

APPROX. 24 IN / 61 CM IN CIRCUMFERENCE

5. Place one sleeve on the circular with the body, matching underarms.

6. Knit the other sleeve and place it on the circular.

7. This is where I decided to change to my longer circular (32 in / 80 cm) because I found it was otherwise too tight to work the raglan. I used the needle as a "magic loop": I drew the cord out into a loop to make it easier to knit. (Read about magic loop knitting on page 113 in the Craft School section.) Continue in stripe sequence as before. Pm at each intersection between body and sleeve and work the raglan shaping as follows: *Knit until 3 sts before marker, k2tog, k1, sl m, k1, ssk*. Rep from * to * at each of the markers. You've now decreased 8 sts around. After I worked 5 decrease rnds, I changed back to the shorter circular. Rep the raglan decrease rnd on every other rnd approx.

20 times. I worked 20 decrease rnds on my sweater, but you might want to adjust the rate of decrease depending on the size of the neck opening and the size of the child's head. Place the sts on a holder (heavy yarn) and pull the sweater on over the child's head. If the opening is too big, work a few more decrease rnds. When you are ready to work the neck, change to dpn and work around in k2, p2 ribbing for ⅝ in / 1.5 cm. **NOTE:** Do not use silver thread on the neck—it's uncomfortably scratchy against soft skin!

8. BO loosely. Seam underarms and then weave in all ends neatly on WS.

9. Soak sweater in lukewarm water and then gently squeeze out excess water. Lay sweater flat and pat out to finished measurements. Leave until completely dry.

HERE'S HOW THE SWEATER LOOKS WHEN YOU PLACE THE SLEEVES ON THE CIRCULAR WITH THE BODY AND ARE ABOUT TO BEGIN THE RAGLAN SHAPING.

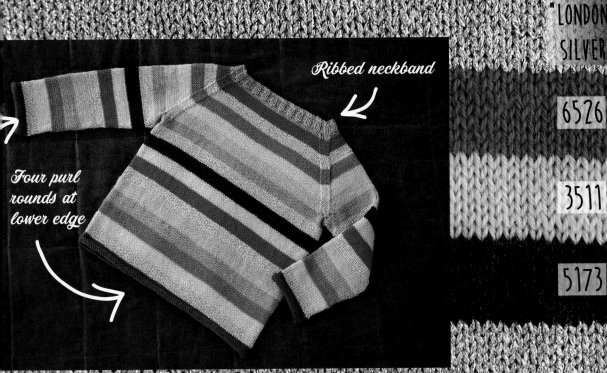

Ribbed neckband

Four purl rounds at lower edge

This hat is very elastic and can fit both a two-year-old and a seven-year-old. It's approximately 9 in / 23 cm high and 17 in / 43 cm in circumference. What's great about it is that you can make it as big or small as you like, because you determine the measurements! All the stitches are knit stitches. Each time I changed colors, I wove in the yarn ends for about 7 stitches so the ends were caught as I worked—and then I didn't have to take care of that later.

MULTICOLORED BABY HAT

HURRAY FOR GLITTER!

ONE SIDE

LEVEL OF DIFFICULTY
Easy

MATERIALS
Yarn (small amounts of each yarn/color):
CYCA #1 (fingering) Sandnes Garn Babyull Lanett (100% Merino wool, 191 yd/175 m / 50 g): 4119, 4312, 2112, 3511, and 5213
CYCA #0 (thread) Sandnes Garn London Gold (60% viscose, 40% polyester, 164 yd/150 m /50 g). Hold 2 strands of London together throughout.
CYCA #3 (DK/light worsted) Sandnes Garn Alpakka (100% alpaca, 120 yd/110 m / 50 g): 2005
CYCA #1 (fingering) Sandnes Garn Sisu (80%

wool/20% polyamide, 191 yd/175 m / 50 g): 4528 heather and 4715
My hat weighed 1¾ oz / 50 g.
Needles: U. S. size 2.5 / 3 mm

TECHNIQUES
Garter stitch (knit all rows) worked back and forth with short rows.

1. CO 60 sts.
2. The hat is worked with short rows. One section consists of 6 rows worked back and forth as follows:
Knit 2 rows over all the sts.

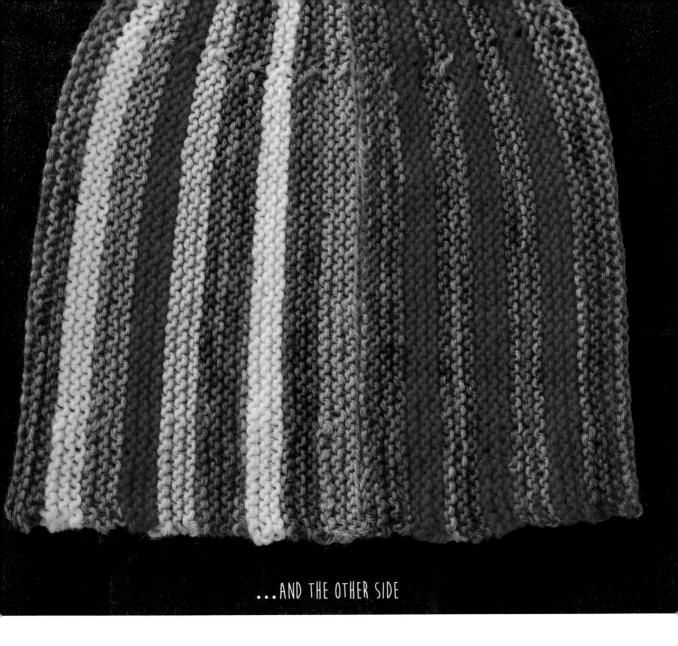

...AND THE OTHER SIDE

Knit 2 rows over the 1st 50 sts—always slip the 1st st purlwise when you turn.

Knit 2 rows over the 1st 40 sts—always slip the 1st st purlwise when you turn.

3. Change colors after each complete 6-row section.

4. BO when you think the hat is big enough in circumference. My hat measured approx. 17 in / 43 cm at the lower edge. Measure around the child's head to make sure the hat will fit.

5. BO, leaving a tail long enough to seam the hat. Join the cast-on and bound-off edges, ending at the top of the hat. Draw the end through the sts at the top and tighten. Knot well and weave ends in neatly on WS.

6. Soak the hat in lukewarm water and then gently squeeze out excess water. Lay flat to dry.

THE SAME HAT FOR ADULTS:

CO 70 sts and knit until the hat is 20½ in / 52 cm in circumference. (The hat pattern is very flexible, and you can easily make it smaller or larger if you want.)

Knit 2 rows over all the sts.

Knit 2 rows over the 1st 60 sts—always slip the 1st st purlwise when you turn.

Knit 2 rows over the 1st 50 sts—always slip the 1st st purlwise when you turn.

CRAFT SCHOOL

KNITTING GAUGE

THE MOST IMPORTANT STEP BEFORE YOU BEGIN KNITTING:

I like to call this "breaking the knitting code," but it's actually called "knitting a gauge swatch"—the meaning is the same. This tells you how many stitches you knitted in 4 in / 10 cm. When you know your gauge with the specific yarn and needles you'll be using, you can easily calculate exactly how many stitches you should cast on, whether you're working without a pattern or just need to match your measurements to a given size.

For that reason, it's essential to knit a gauge swatch and count how many stitches you knitted in 4 in / 10 cm. Believe me, I know how it is when you come home with some new yarn! You just want to get going right away, and can't be bothered to knit a swatch. But that just means the yarn and needles will end up tossed aside in frustration, because the measurements were wrong and you had to rip out everything ... and it happens more often than not that the garment you were so excited to work on ends up in the pile with all the other UFOs (Un-Finished Objects). Don't let this happen to you: the most important lesson any knitter can learn is that you MUST knit a gauge swatch before you begin!

How to knit and measure a gauge swatch:
Knit a swatch larger than 4 x 4 in / 10 x 10 cm. Lay a measuring tape on the swatch and count how many stitches fit into 4 in / 10 cm. From there, you can calculate the stitch count for almost anything! For example, let's say there are 22 stitches in 4 in / 10 cm, and you want to knit a sweater with a chest measurement of 49¾ in / 126 cm, which means 24¾ in / 63 cm for the front and 24¾ in / 63 cm for the back. Calculate the stitch count you need as follows:
22 stitches divided by 4 in = 5.5 sts per inch x 24.75 inches = 136 sts each for front and back / 22 stitches divided by 10 cm = 2.2 sts per cm x 63 cm = 138.6 stitches. You can round up or down as necessary—if you're working with a pattern stitch or motif, pick the nearest multiple of the repeat required. (Due to rounding when converting centimeters to inches, stitch counts may be slightly different, but not usually by the span of an entire pattern repeat; you should end up with approximately the same answer no matter which you use.)
Best of all, you'll have a garment with the correct measurements. Hurray!

SEWING INVISIBLE SEAMS

When you're sewing two pieces together—say, for example, the shoulders on a garment—it's best to use an "invisible" seam. It goes without saying that you should use the same yarn as for the rest of the garment; I used a contrast color here to make the seam visible, for illustrative purposes only! Kitchener stitch is equivalent to duplicate stitch: you just follow the path a knitted stitch would take. In this picture, you can see how you make the join. Insert the needle diagonally under/through a whole stitch on one side, and then insert the needle diagonally under a whole stitch on the other side. Continue the same way, working back and forth through the stitches. Don't tighten the yarn too much! You can even out the join by very carefully steam pressing the seam under a damp pressing cloth, on the wrong side of the work.

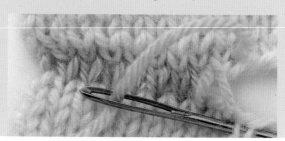

MAGIC LOOP

I like to knit with the so-called "magic loop" method when I'm knitting in the round on small pieces, or working on sections that are a little too tight for knitting in the round on a short circular. A magic loop means that you draw out the soft cord of the circular needle into one or two loops (the photo to the left shows two loops) between two stitches. Knitting with a long circular works well for knitting in the round on a garment with a smaller circumference. For example, knitting ragg socks with a set of five double-pointed needles can be difficult—it's easier to manage a single 24 in / 60 cm circular, magic-loop style. I often use a very long circular in a magic loop when I knit a raglan yoke.

THUMB GUSSET

See the explanation of a thumb gusset in the basic mitten pattern on page 87. The photos below show how the thumb gusset looks when you've completed it and placed the stitches on scrap yarn. This holds the stitches while you knit the rest of the mitten, until you're ready to come back and knit the thumb. The photo on the left shows the gusset lying flat. You can clearly see the V-shape. The photo on the right shows how the gusset looks when folded, the way it'll look when the mitten is finished.

INVISIBLE INCREASES

There's always a strand between two stitches that you can pick up and work a new stitch into, creating an "invisible" increase. Pick up the strand with the tip of the left needle and knit into the back loop with the right needle. Now you've avoided a hole in the fabric! This is called a M1 or "make 1" increase.

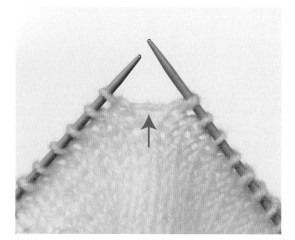

HERE IS THE STRAND TO PICK UP.

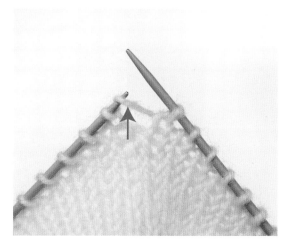

PICK UP THE STRAND WITH THE TIP OF THE LEFT NEEDLE.

FRENCH KNOTS

Bring the thread up to the right side of the fabric and wrap the thread 3 times around the needle tip (see upper photo). Point the needle tip straight down about 1⁄16 in / 2 mm from the spot where the thread came up. Tighten the thread around the needle (see lower photo) and push the needle down through the fabric. Draw the thread tight with care so the French knot is plump and pretty!

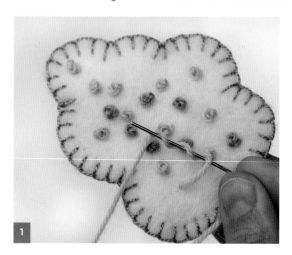

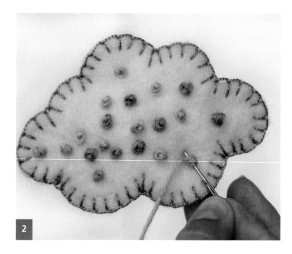

EMBROIDERED STITCHES = DUPLICATE STITCH

Embroidered stitches are both fun and practical since they can substitute for pattern knitting to a limited extent. The yarn follows the same path as a knitted stitch would. Bring the needle up at the base of the V of a stitch. Draw the yarn up carefully and then bring the needle diagonally through the center of the stitch directly over the stitch you're working with (if you look closely, you'll see that knitted stitches hang together at that point). Now insert the needle down in the same place where the yarn came up, also at the base of the V. For the photos below, I embroidered with a slightly heavier yarn than for the knitting.

3. THE NEEDLES GOES BACK TO THE WRONG SIDE AT THE BASE OF THE V:

DECREASES— LEFT-LEANING DECREASE = K2TOG THROUGH BACK LOOPS

When decreasing on each side of a marker, you work a knit-two-together (k2tog) on each side of the marker. It'll look smoothest if you make a left-leaning decrease before the marker. There are several ways to do this! The photo here shows how to knit two together through back loops (k2tog tbl). Insert the right needle through the 2 sts as shown in the photo. Alternatively, you can work ssk—slip, slip, knit. Insert the needle knitwise into the 1st st on left needle and slip to right needle; slip the next stitch the same way. Now knit the sts together through the back loops.

CHOOSING COLORS

Whether you're designing furnishings, clothing, or accessories, you'll need one or more color cards—or you can make your own! I love making color cards, because I love colors. I know that many people think it's diffi-cult to come up with their own colorways to use for knitting, but I've learned to consider it a fun challenge. Cut out some cardboard or card stock about 2 x 3¼ in / 5 x 8 cm wide, and wind yarn around the cards (see the photo below). It should be obvious that if you hold yarn from two balls of yarn side by side, it won't be nearly as easy to see the effect of the color combination as when you wrap the yarns around something flat.

TIP:
If you're knitting or crocheting
with many colors, it can be a chore to weave
in all the yarn ends… So don't wait and stick
yourself with that boring task at the end—weave
in the yarns as you work instead! I guarantee
you'll be happier than if you wait until the knitting
or crochet is almost done.

HOW TO FELT WOOL

Felting wool essentially means that you "shock" the wool so much that it shrinks. I lay carded wool on a washboard—a thin layer horizontally and then a thin layer vertically. I continue with 5-6 layers in alternating directions, depending on how thick I want the final fabric. I then pour some soap and warm water (2 tablespoons soap per quart / liter of water) into a plastic bucket. Saturate the wool with the soapy water and then begin massaging the wool lightly in a circular motion with your fingertips. When you see that the wool is starting to adhere to itself, you can massage it with your whole hand. Drain your current water away and add more fresh soapy water. Continue to massage and knead the wool. Take it up and twist it between your hands and work it hard. If you have an old washboard, that's perfect for felting! When you're satisfied with the felting and the wool feels sturdy and well-joined, rinse out the piece with water until the soap is all gone and then leave it out to dry. If you need a better explanation for felting, there are several books on the subject and many good instructional videos on the internet.

KNIT - KNIT - KNIT - KNIT - KNIT -

KNITTING CAN ALSO BE A STARTING POINT FOR FELTING AS LONG AS THE YARN IS PURE WOOL. TWEED YARN MAKES IT EVEN LIVELIER.

MAKING POMPOMS

1. Cut a circle out of cardboard or heavy card stock (for example, a cereal box). The larger the circle you cut out, the larger the finished pompom. Draw a new circle at the center of the first one and cut it out to make a "doughnut" hole. Make another template the same way and hold the two together.
2. Begin by wrapping the yarn around the templates, through the holes at the centers. I wrap 4 strands at once to make it go faster. If you use several colors, you'll have a tweedy pompom. Don't use too little yarn because that makes the pompom uneven and sparse! The more yarn you use, the puffier and fuller the finished pompom will be.
3. When the centers of the templates are completely filled with yarn, insert the tip of a pair of scissors between the edges of the two templates and cut the outer ends of the yarn open.
4. Slide some strong thread between the templates and tighten to hold the yarn securely. Tie a strong knot. Now you can remove the yarn from the templates.
5. Carefully trim the pompom with sharp scissors until it's round and poofy. **NOTE:** It's impossible to trim a pompom neatly with dull scissors—always use the sharpest scissors you can find!

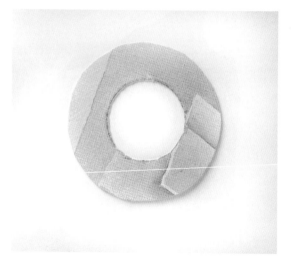

MAKING A CLASSIC TASSEL

1. Wrap yarn around a piece of cardboard that's a little wider than the length you want for the finished tassel. Carefully pull the yarn off the cardboard and wrap a new yarn end around the tassel a short distance from the top so the tassel has a "neck" and a "head." Knot the yarn at the back of the tassel.
2. Draw a strand of yarn through the head of the tassel and tie a knot at the top.
3. Cut the yarn ends open at the bottom of the tassel; trim ends with sharp scissors.

KNITTING BASICS: CASTING ON STITCHES

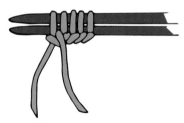

1. Make a slip knot as shown above for the 1st stitch placed on the needle(s). Make sure you leave a long enough end for the entire cast-on.

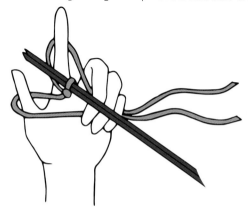

2. Tighten the yarn loop around the needle(s)—but not too much! (You can also cast on with only one needle if you prefer.) Hold the yarn and needles as shown in the drawing.

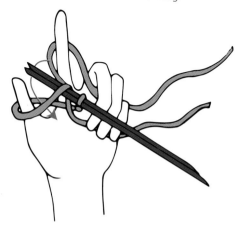

3. Catch the "thumb yarn" (the lower strand) with the needle(s). Catch the "index finger yarn" and draw it through/between the thumb strands. Slip the yarn off the thumb and tighten both ends; you now have a new stitch on the needle(s).

4. The picture above shows how the stitches look when you've cast on a row of them. If you used two needles, carefully remove one and begin knitting! When you cast on over two needles, the stitches are looser and more flexible. You can, of course, use only one needle, but in that case you should make sure you cast on more loosely.

Binding off (= British casting off):
Knit 2 stitches. Pass the right stitch over the left one on the right needle. Knit another stitch and pass the right stitch over the left one on the right needle. Repeat this step until all the stitches have been bound off. When, for example, you are binding off on a collar, you need to bind off loosely, so the edge doesn't draw or roll in.

KNITTING ABBREVIATIONS and TERMS

BO	bind off (= British cast off)	p2tog	purl 2 together = 1 st decreased
cm	centimeter(s)	pb&b	purl into back and then front of the same stitch = 1 st increased
CO	cast on		
dpn	double-pointed needles		
est	established	pm	place marker
g	gram(s)	rem	remain(s)(ing)
in	inch(es)	rnd(s)	round(s)
k	knit	RS	right side
kf&b	knit into the front and then into the back of the same stitch = 1 st increased	sl	slip
		sl m	slip marker
		st(s)	stitch(es)
		tbl	through back loop(s)
k2tog	knit 2 together = right-leaning decrease, 1 st decreased	WS	wrong side
		yd	yard(s)
m	meter(s)		
mm	millimeter(s)	garter stitch	
ndl(s)	needle(s)	knit every row if working back and forth or alternate knit and purl rnds in the round	
oz	ounce(s)		
p	purl		
		reverse stockinette	
		knit on the wrong side and purl on the right side	

HOW TO KNIT

You'll find loads of good videos on the internet to show you how to knit!

THE RIGHT SIDE LOOKS LIKE THIS

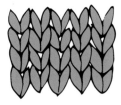

THE WRONG SIDE LOOKS LIKE THIS

MAKING KNIT STITCHES

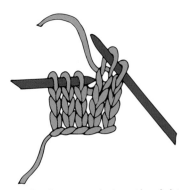

1: Insert the right needle into the 1st stitch on the left needle as shown (from left to right). Catch the yarn behind the left needle and bring it through the stitch to the front.

2: Slip the new stitch to the right needle.

MAKING PURL STITCHES

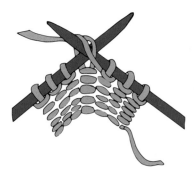

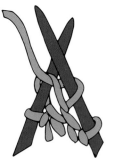

1: Hold the yarn over the left needle in front of work. Insert the right needle from the wrong side (under the yarn) through the 1st stitch on the left needle (from right to left and back to front). Throw the yarn around the right needle and position the loop in front of the left needle.

2: Bring the right needle with the yarn loop back through the stitch on the left needle so it makes a stitch on the right needle. Let the stitch slide off the left needle.

CROCHET BASICS

You'll find loads of good videos on the internet to show you how to crochet!

Chain stitch (ch):

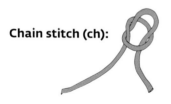

1. Make a slip knot as shown above. Place the loop on the crochet hook and tighten (but not too much!) so the stitch sits in the correct position.

2. Draw the yarn through the stitch loop on the hook as shown in the drawing.

3. Here's a chain made of several chain stitches.

Single crochet (sc) = British double crochet:

1. After you've made a foundation chain with chain stitches, turn the chain and insert the hook into the 2nd chain from the hook. Catch the yarn around the hook as shown above.

2. Bring the yarn through the 1st stitch so you now have 2 loops on the hook. Wrap the yarn around the hook and bring it through both loops.

3. Now 1 loop is left on the hook and the single crochet stitch is complete. Insert the hook through the next chain stitch and make a new single crochet stitch.

Slip stitch (sl st):

Yarn around the hook and directly through the stitch and the loop on the hook to make one slip stitch.

Ring:

To make a ring of chain stitches, join the last chain stitch to the 1st with 1 slip stitch, as shown in the drawing above.

Crochet around a ring:

When, for example, crocheting double crochet around a ring, insert the hook into the ring (below the chain stitches) and bring the yarn through as shown above.

Half double crochet (hdc) = British half treble

Yarn around the hook, insert the hook through the next stitch, yarn around the hook, and bring the yarn through all 3 loops on the hook—as shown in the drawing to the right. Now you've completed a half double crochet stitch.

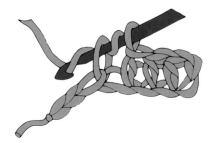

Double crochet (dc) = British treble

Yarn around the hook, insert the hook through the next stitch, yarn around the hook (now there are 3 loops on the hook), and bring the yarn through the 1st 2 loops on the hook—as shown in the drawing to the right. Two loops are left on the hook. Yarn around the hook and through the remaining 2 loops. Now you've completed a double crochet stitch.

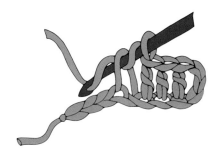

Treble crochet (tr) = British double treble

Yarn around the hook twice, insert the hook through the next stitch, yarn around the hook (now there are 4 loops on the hook), and bring the yarn through the 1st 2 loops on the hook—as shown in the drawing to the right. Three loops are left on the hook. Yarn around the hook and through the next 2 loops; yarn around hook and through remaining 2 loops. Now you've completed a treble crochet stitch.

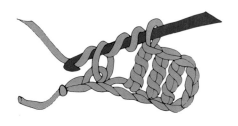

CROCHET ABBREVIATIONS

ch	chain	hdc	half double crochet (= British half treble)
dc	double crochet (= British treble crochet)	pm	place marker
		rem	remain(s)(ing)
est	established	rnd(s)	round(s)
gr	group (several stitches worked into the same stitch or loop)	RS	right side
		sc	single crochet (= British double crochet)

sl	slip
sl m	slip marker
st(s)	stitch(es)
tr	treble crochet (= British double treble)
WS	wrong side
crab stitch	work single crochet from left to right

GRANNY SQUARES

ROUND 1 WITH COLOR 1

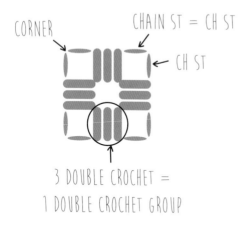

CORNER

CHAIN ST = CH ST

CH ST

3 DOUBLE CROCHET =
1 DOUBLE CROCHET GROUP

ROUND 2 WITH COLOR 2

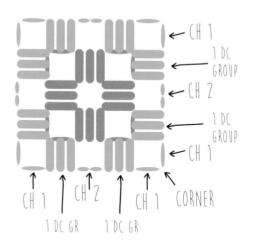

CH 1

1 DC GROUP

CH 2

1 DC GROUP

CH 1

CH 1   CH 2   CH 1   CORNER

1 DC GR   1 DC GR

ROUND 3 WITH COLOR 3

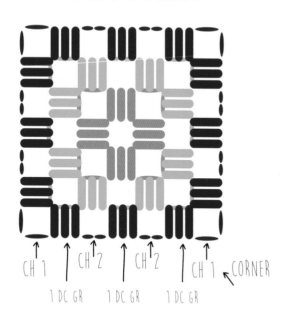

CH 1   CH 2   CH 2   CH 1   CORNER

1 DC GR   1 DC GR   1 DC GR

ROUND 4 WITH COLOR 4

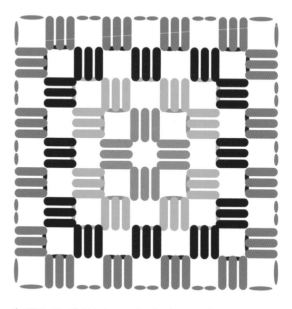

CROCHET THE 4TH ROUND AS FOR THE PREVIOUS ROUND BUT WITH 1 MORE DC GROUP BETWEEN THE CORNERS. DON'T FORGET THAT ONLY THE 1ST SQUARE IS COMPLETE AS SHOWN ABOVE. ALL SUBSEQUENT SQUARES ARE JOINED TO OTHER SQUARES ON THE LAST ROUND.

TIP: ON THE INTERNET, YOU'LL FIND LOTS OF VIDEOS SHOWING HOW TO MAKE GRANNY SQUARES!

HOW TO CROCHET GRANNY SQUARES

1. Color 1: Ch 5 and join into a ring with 1 sl st into 1st ch. Ch 3 (= 1st dc), 2 dc around ring (= 1st dc gr), ch 2. Work (3 dc around ring, ch 2) 3 times = a total of 4 dc groups. End with 1 sl st into top of ch 3 at beginning of rnd (see photo above). Cut yarn and fasten off.

2. Color 2: Begin at a corner, attaching yarn around a ch loop. Ch 3 + 2 dc around ch loop at corner = 1st dc gr. Ch 2, 3 dc gr in same ch loop, ch 2. Work (3 dc gr, ch 2) two times in each of the next 3 corners = 8 dc groups around. There is always a ch 2 between each dc gr. End rnd with 1 sl st into top of ch 3 at beginning of rnd. Cut yarn and fasten off. The photo above shows 4 dc gr, 2 in each corner.

3. Color 3: Begin at a corner, attaching yarn around a ch loop. (Ch 3, 2 dc, ch 2, 3 dc, ch 2) in corner ch loop = 2 dc gr in corner. Work (3 dc gr, ch 2) in the center ch loop of previous rnd. Continue around with 2 dc gr in each corner and 1 dc gr in each ch loop between corners + ch 2 between each dc gr. End with 1 sl st into top of ch 3 at beginning of rnd. Cut yarn and fasten off.

4. Color 4: Work as for Rnd 3, but now there are 2 ch loops on each side instead of 1 between the corners. For the 1st square only, work all around the square, ending with 1 sl st into top of ch 3 at beginning of rnd.
For subsequent squares, join as you work: Align the squares corner to corner, work 3 dc in corner in new square, ch 1, 1 sl st around the corner ch loop of the other square...

get lost

in

beautiful

yarn ♡

METALLIC YARN
♡

5. ... and then work the next dc group in the corner, ch 1 and 1 sl st around the other square's ch loop.

6. Continue crocheting the squares to each other the same way: between each dc gr, work ch 1 and 1 sl st around the other square's ch loop. When you get to a corner, there are 2 dc groups to join.

7. Continue around the square and end the rnd with 1 sl st into top of ch 3 at beginning of rnd. Cut yarn and fasten off.

8. Blanket edging: Attach yarn in the ch loop at corner, ch 3, 2 dc, ch 2 and then repeat (3 dc, ch 2) in every ch loop around, but at each corner work 2 3-dc gr as before (with ch 2 between groups). End the rnd with 1 sl st into top of ch 3 at beginning of rnd. You can repeat this round until edging is desired width; use as many colors as you like. Cut yarn and fasten off.

CROCHETED HEXAGONS

1. Color 1: Ch 5 and join into a ring with 1 sl st into 1st ch. Ch 3 (= 1st dc), 11 dc around ring = 12 dc total.

2. End with 1 sl st into top of ch 3 at beginning of rnd.

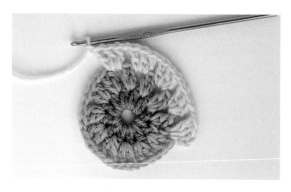

3. Color 2: (Ch 3, 1 dc, ch 1) between 2 dc and then work (2 dc, ch 1) between each dc of previous rnd. End with 1 sl st into top of ch 3 at beginning of rnd.

4. Color 3: (Ch 3, 2 dc, ch 1) between 2 dc and then work (3 dc, ch 1) between each dc group of previous rnd. End with 1 sl st into top of ch 3 at beginning of rnd.

5. Color 4: Work (1 sl st in ch of previous rnd, ch 4) around. End with 1 sl st into 1st sl st.

6. Work a dc gr (beginning 1st gr with ch 3) in each ch loop. *Work a corner: (3 dc, ch 1, 3 dc, ch 1) in ch loop. In next ch loop, work (3 dc, ch 1)*; rep * to * around = 6 corners!

NOTE: For the 1st hexagon only, work all around the hexagon, ending with 1 sl st into top of ch 3 at beginning of rnd.

For subsequent hexagons, join as you work—see next series of photos.

7. To join hexagons, align two hexagons corner to corner as shown in the photo above. In 1st hexagon, work 3 dc, ch 1, and then, in corner of adjacent hexagon, work 1 sl st.

8. After working 3 dc more and ch 1 in the same ch loop of 1st hexagon, work 1 sl into ch loop of adjacent hexagon.

9. Continue joining the hexagons. In every other ch loop, work 6 dc (= 2 dc groups separated by ch 1) to make a corner, alternating with (3 dc, ch 1) in next ch loop. The photo above shows how 3 hexagons are joined: Work 3 dc, ch 1, 1 sl st through both of the two other hexagons' corner ch loops, 3 dc again in the same ch loop.

10. Here is the finished hexagon joined to two others. End with 1 sl st into top of ch 3 at beginning of rnd.

HOW DO YOU DYE YARN?

READ ENTIRELY THROUGH THE INSTRUCTIONS BEFORE YOU BEGIN for an overview of what you'll be doing and how to find the tools and materials you'll need. I use a powder form of yarn dye that's sold in hobby shops in small packets. Make sure the dye you choose is formulated for wool, not cotton, if you're going to dye wool yarn. Also, check to make sure any wool yarn is 100% wool. Acrylic and polyester don't take up the color from wool dyes! Read the packet specifications carefully. I use single use plastic cups and spoons if I want to blend different shades before I drip the color onto the yarn or dip the yarn into a color bath. Sometimes I scoop concentrated powder onto the shaft of a plastic spoon and drizzle the powder directly onto the yarn where I want it. The powder I use is very concentrated, and you might be shocked at how strong the color looks at first—but it does tone down as the yarn dries.

The most important factor when dyeing wool yarn is to ensure the wool doesn't felt. You must handle the yarn very carefully and avoid large and sudden changes of temperature. When you've soaked the yarn and are ready to put it in the dyepot, the water should be the same temperature as the yarn. Don't put lukewarm wool yarn into boiling hot water! The same applies to the yarn when it's at 175°F / 80°C and ready to dye—it'll be a catastrophe if you rinse wool yarn in cold water right after it's been in the hot dyebath.

1. I begin by winding the yarn into a skein on a skein winder. Tie several strands around the skein so the yarn won't felt and tangle. It's important to tie the strands loosely enough for the dye to penetrate the yarn.

2. Place all the yarn bundles in lukewarm water and leave them long enough to thoroughly saturate. Press the yarn into the water and make sure none of the yarn sticks out of the water.

3. Lift the wet yarn out of the water and transfer it to a wide dyepot. Add a little water—but not enough to cover the yarn completely. Add vinegar if needed; read and follow the instructions on your dye packet. The type of dye I use suggests vinegar as a fixative, but if the dye you're using recommends something different, use that instead.

4. Place the dyepot on the stove and put in a thermometer—but don't let the thermometer hit the bottom of the pan. Take the temperature in the center of the yarn/water. Keep an eye on the thermometer; the contents of the dyepot have to be hot enough that the dye adheres to the fiber, but not boiling!

5. Add the dye at various places on the yarn. Dye spreads out in water; if you add too much water, the dye will spread all over the yarn instead of adhering in specific places. With less water, you can better control the placement of your colors. When the water is once again clear (meaning the yarn has absorbed all of the first dye application), you can add the next color. Continue until the yarn is the colorway you want. The instructions for my dye say that I should keep the bath at a certain temperature for 20 minutes—check to see whether your dye has similar requirements for the dye to be colorfast.

6. Use a sieve to remove the yarn from the dyepot so you don't burn yourself, and then put it in a sink to cool before you rinse the yarn. Rinse the skeins several times in lukewarm water. Gently squeeze out the excess water and lay the yarn to dry.

7. When the yarn is completely dry, untie the ties around the skeins and rewind the yarn on a skein winder. I use an electric winder, but you can also wind by hand.

TIPS

TRY KNITTING EVERY OTHER ROW WITH 2 DIFFERENT COLORS OF YARN. IF YOU DON'T WANT TWEEDY YARN, JUST MIX THE COLORS YOU WANT ON THE YARN DIRECTLY IN THE POT AND THEN ADD THE YARN—IT WILL BE ONE COLOR, BUT THAT COLOR WILL BE YOUR OWN.

HOW TO DYE
MULTI-SHADED YARN

FOR THESE SKEINS, I BLENDED PINK, RED, BLUE, YELLOW, BROWN, NAVY BLUE, AND GRAY—I MIXED THE SHADES AND THEN ADDED A LITTLE MORE COLOR HERE AND THERE!

1. I use Smart yarn from Sandnes Garn when I want to dye yarn.

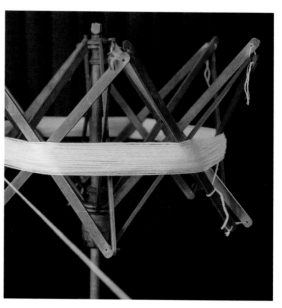

2. Wind the yarn from the ball into a skein on a skein winder.

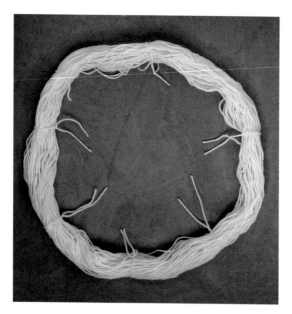

3. Use several short strands of yarn to make several ties around the skein; knot *loosely*. Remove skein from winder.

4. When the yarn is thoroughly saturated with water, transfer it to a dyepot and add enough water to cover the yarn halfway. Add vinegar or the recommended fixative for the dye so the colors will be colorfast.

5. I pour dyes into plastic cups (one use only) so I can mix the colors. I drop the dye onto the yarn or sprinkle the dye powder directly onto the yarn.

6. Wait a while between different colors so the yarn has time to completely absorb one color before you start the next. Here I've dyed with brown and gray and am now dribbling on the navy blue.

7. Now the navy blue has been added.

8. For this yarn, I didn't want much white showing, so I continued to add more colors until I was satisfied with the result. After all the dye was added, the yarn needed to stay at the recommended temperature for 20 minutes.

BEAUTIFUL THINGS
DON'T ASK FOR
ATTENTION

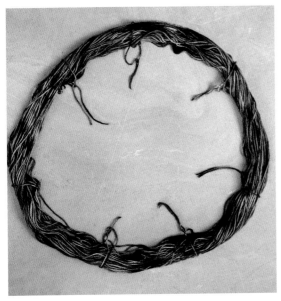

9. When the yarn is ready, let it cool and then rinse it well but carefully so it doesn't felt. Gently squeeze out the excess water and let yarn dry completely.

10. Here's how the yarn looks after it is dry.

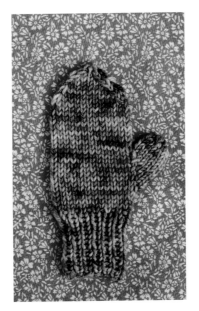

Here is another color combination: purple, blue, and red.

I used yellow, pink, red, and blue, blending the colors so there were many, many different nuances!

For this mitten, I used purple, blue, yellow, and red.

yarn is like
CHOCOLATE
you can never have too much

---- MOHAIR ♡

Thank you, my dear...

ACKNOWLEDGMENTS

Photography Leif Hansen
You took the best photos, as always! It such a pleasure to work with you.
See more of Leif's photos at: www.leifhansen.se

The staff at Sandnes Garn, and specifically Eva Ølberg and Gry Geelmuyden—such lovely yarn! Check out Sandnes' home page: www.sandnes-garn.no

The models Astrid and Alice—
You were wonderful—love you!

My beloved family: Casper, Nils, and Alice—you are the best.

And a special thank-you to everyone who buys my book so that I can continue to do exactly what I love doing most!

If you want to see more of my work, find me on Instagram: @fridapontendesign.

YARN SUPPLIERS

Sandnes yarns may be purchased in North America (with international shipping charges) from:

Scandinavian Knitting Design
www.scandinavianknittingdesign.com

A variety of additional and substitute yarns are available from:
Webs—America's Yarn Store
75 Service Center Road
Northampton, MA 01060
800-367-9327
www.yarn.com

LoveKnitting.com
www.loveknitting.com/us

If you are unable to obtain any of the yarn used in this book, it can be replaced with a yarn of a similar weight and composition. Please note, however, the finished projects may vary slightly from those shown, depending on the yarn used.
Try www.yarnsub.com for suggestions.
For more information on selecting or substituting yarn, contact your local yarn shop or an online store; they are familiar with all types of yarns and would be happy to help you. Additionally, the online knitting community at Ravelry.com has forums where you can post questions about specific yarns. Yarns come and go so quickly these days and there are so many beautiful yarns available.

SO MU

...SO LIT